THE VALUATION OF SHARES
AND THE
EFFICIENT-MARKETS THEORY

STUDIES IN FINANCE AND ACCOUNTING

General Editors: M. J. Barron and D. W. Pearce

Published

Michael Firth: MANAGEMENT OF WORKING CAPITAL
Michael Firth: THE VALUATION OF SHARES AND THE EFFICIENT-MARKETS THEORY
Kenneth Midgley and Ronald Burns: THE CAPITAL MARKET: ITS NATURE AND SIGNIFICANCE

Forthcoming

M. J. Barron: BUSINESS FINANCE THEORY
M. J. Barron: MATRIX MODELS FOR ACCOUNTING
Brian Quinn: MULTINATIONAL BUSINESS FINANCE AND ACCOUNTING
T. Ryan: PORTFOLIO ANALYSIS
R. W. Scapens: ACCOUNTING IN AN INFLATIONARY ENVIRONMENT
Charles Sutcliffe: ECONOMICS VERSUS ACCOUNTANCY

The Valuation of Shares and the Efficient-Markets Theory

MICHAEL FIRTH

*Lecturer in the Department of Accountancy and Business Law,
University of Stirling*

First published 1977 by
THE MACMILLAN PRESS LTD
London and Basingstoke
Associated companies in New York Dublin
Melbourne Johannesburg and Madras

ISBN 0 333 21409 9 (hard cover)
0 333 21410 2 (paper cover)

Typeset, printed and bound
in Great Britain by
REDWOOD BURN LIMITED
Trowbridge & Esher

Contents

General Editors' Preface

The last few years have been very exciting for research in finance and accounting. An enormous amount has happened, and in many cases traditional thinking and traditional solutions have been completely overthrown. At the same time it is quite clear that research into the theory and, perhaps even more important, into British empirical evidence, will continue to accumulate rapidly. While this is fine for the researcher in his detailed specialist world, it is not so good for the student who wants to acquire a relatively straightforward but up-to-date overview of the subject.

The 'Macmillan Studies in Finance and Accounting' set out to provide short, reasonably critical surveys of the developments within the various specialist areas of business finance and accounting. The emphasis in each study is upon recent work, but each topic will generally be placed in a historical context so that the reader may see the logical development of thought through time. Selected bibliographies are provided to guide readers to more extensive works. Each study aims at a brief treatment of the salient problems in order to avoid clouding the issues in too much detailed argument.

Unfortunately it is inevitable that in a few areas the level of mathematics will be rather near the limit for some students. This is because the rigorous methods of statistics, econometrics and mathematical economics have made a considerable contribution to the research achievements in the subject. Thus, although all the authors in the series have tried hard to make their presentation as lucid as possible, there is a point beyond which mathematical arguments cannot be explained non-mathematically except at a superficial level. Nevertheless intuition can go a long way and many students, even with very little mathematical background, have found that the intrinsic fascination of the subject more than compensates for the occasional difficulty.

M. J. Barron
D. W. Pearce

CHAPTER 1

The Role of the Stock Market

The major socio-economic role of a stock exchange is the valuing of securities and the provision of a well-run market-place where investors can buy and sell shares. The 'proper' valuation of securities is important as it provides signals for the allocation of scarce capital resources. Thus investment funds are channelled towards those companies which can use them most profitably (and, from the viewpoint of a capitalist economy, most usefully). The provision of a well-run market-place – along with accurate pricing – is required if individuals are going to invest in private enterprise, either via some investment institution, for example a unit trust, or on their own. If the market is not well run and securities are incorrectly priced, then many individuals will stop investing and this will seriously reduce the availability of funds to expanding companies.

The accurate pricing of securities is essential if scarce capital resources (i.e. cash) are to be used most efficiently (i.e. profitably); and the efficiency of the allocation of scarce resources is a major determinant of a nation's growth and standard of living perform-ance. If the stock exchange significantly fails in its pricing of shares and if the running of the share-exchange mechanism is poor, then the market will become very speculative. This must eventually lead to a more controlled economy, i.e. the Government taking over the function of the stock exchange.

The allocation of scarce capital resources is influenced in both a direct and an indirect manner by the stock market. Direct influence comes from the new-issue and rights-issue markets. Here the com-pany is seeking additional outside finance. Whether such finance is forthcoming, and at what price, depends upon the stock market's assessment of the firm involved and on its prospects. Although the stock market's reaction to new issues and rights issues tends to go in cycles, there are still significant differences in the reaction to individual issues, for example some firms have found it impossible to raise new finance on the stock market whilst others, at the same point in time, have found it to be quite easy. Thus the stock market does exert influence on whether companies can raise fresh finance.

Indirect influence on resource allocation is effected by the stock market in the form of share prices and investment comment. If a company has performed badly and if the immediate prospects appear poor, then the firm will almost certainly be showing a relatively poor share price performance. This will deter or prevent the firm from going to the stock market to raise new capital and in addition may attract takeover interest. Potential takeover bids are likely as the bidders will be hoping to improve the returns on the assets of the firm, which are at a low level.

In order that share prices are correctly valued and that the share-exchange mechanism is well run, we need a perfect market, the major requirements of which are:

(*a*) homogeneity of the goods;
(*b*) many buyers and sellers;
(*c*) freedom of entry and exit;
(*d*) unlimited supplies of stocks and shares; and
(*e*) perfect knowledge.

The major stock exchanges of the world have broadly met the first four requirements such that they impose no serious constraints on the functioning of the stock market.[1] Specifically, there is homogeneity of goods; one ordinary share in Marks and Spencer confers the same rights as any other ordinary share in Marks and Spencer. There are many buyers and sellers in the stock market and there is active dealing in all but the smallest company securities. Whilst there are transaction costs incurred in buying and selling securities, these rates are known and smallish in magnitude. As such they do not impose serious drawbacks on the stock market and there are no other constraints affecting freedom of entry and exit. Although supplies of shares are limited as companies have fixed capitals, it is not felt that this imposes great limitations in the workings of the market. For the smallest limited companies there is sometimes a shortage of stock and at other times there may be a shortage of buyers and sellers. For medium- and large-size firms, however, the institutional arrangements of the stock exchange do not appear to limit its effectiveness as a market-place.

The fifth condition, perfect knowledge, requires that all knowledge relating to the value of a company (for example future earnings, asset values) is known and that this knowledge is accurately conveyed in share prices. Obviously this requirement is not met in the case of ordinary shares. However the major stock markets of the world, i.e. those that have 'succeeded', have managed to provide 'reasonable' share pricing. A major aim of this book is to show how 'reasonable' the pricing has been and how this has been arrived at.

Summary Statistics Relating to the U.K. Stock Market

The following tables present a few statistics which show the value of assets quoted in the London stock market, the amount of finance raised by U.K. companies on the stock market, and the spread of ownership of U.K. ordinary shares. These statistics indicate that the stock market has achieved a fairly important position in valuing and financing industrial, commercial and financial ventures and has obtained this financing via millions of investors, some wealthy, many not so.

Table 1.1 shows both the nominal and market values of all securities quoted on the London stock exchange as at 31 December 1975. The market value of the ordinary share capital of U.K. registered companies comes to £42,491 million – clearly an enormous sum. As a comparison the value of U.K. ordinary share capital at the end of 1966 amounted to £27,148 million. Although the market value of the ordinary shares do not equate to replacement cost or the current market value of the assets, they do represent the market's opinion of the economic value of the net assets of firms. Table 1.1 also shows that considerable funds have been raised by U.K. firms via loan stocks and preference-share capital (given by the nominal capital heading). The market values of these securities have fallen below the nominal value, showing that the interest rates offered have failed to account for the levels of inflation experienced.

As described previously, the stock market exerts direct influence on the allocation of capital resources. Table 1.2 shows the sources of finance of quoted U.K. companies and the classification 'proceeds from the issue of loan and share capital' represents the stock market's

Table 1.1

Nominal and market values of securities quoted on the London stock exchange as at 31 December 1975

	Number of securities	Nominal amount (£m.)	Percentage total	Market valuation (£m.)	Percentage total
Gilt-edged and foreign stocks	1528	42239	55·9	30989	12·4
Loan capital U.K.-registered	2329	6610	8·8	3977 ⎫	
Loan capital non U.K. or Irish-registered	39	259 ⎫		176 ⎬	1·7
Loan capital Republic of Ireland	24	49 ⎭	0·4	47 ⎭	
Preference and preferred capital U.K.-registered	1472	1088	1·4	495 ⎫	
Preference and preferred capital non U.K. or Irish-registered	69	172 ⎫		212 ⎬	0·3
Preference and preferred capital Republic of Ireland	69	17 ⎭	0·2	9 ⎭	
Ordinary share capital U.K.-registered	2820	13138	17·4	42491	17·0
Ordinary share capital non U.K. or Irish-registered	362	11896	15·7	161820	64·6
Ordinary share capital Republic of Ireland	94	146	0·2	384 ⎫	
Shares of no par value non U.K.-registered	25			9845 ⎭	4·0
		75614		250445	

NOTES: Loan capital includes convertible securities; ordinary share capital includes deferred share capital.

Source: Stock Exchange Fact Book (31 December 1975).

direct contribution. Whilst this contribution has declined in percentage terms, the total amount raised in 1973 of £564 million is clearly a substantial amount. In addition the raising of equity capital usually enables short-term credit to be expanded as lenders often limit their loans to some percentage of the permanent (equity) capital. Sometimes of course it is the very largeness of the short-term credit which forces a firm to go to the stock market to get more funds, i.e. to broaden the equity base. For young dynamic firms the stock market often provides the only source of finance for major expansions. During recent years this has become a very major role for the stock market. Both Tables 1.1 and 1.2 have

Table 1.2

Sources of finance of quoted companies

	2109 (1966)		1993 (1967)		1829 (1968)		1701 (1969)		1308 (1970)		1239 (1971)		1168 (1972)		1116 (1973)	
Number of companies	£m.	% total	£m.	% total	£m.	% total	£m.	% total	£m.	% total	£m.	% total	£m.	% total	£m.	% total
Proceeds from the issue of loan and share capital	482	20·2	519	19·3	421	13·5	343	9·2	274	6·9	505	18	440	8·8	564	6·4
Retained profit plus depreciation	1395	59·3	1615	60·1	1839	58·8	1841	49·2	1988	50·3	2241	79·6	3046	61	3637	41·7
Increase in short-term credit	481	20·5	552	20·6	870	27·7	1556	41·6	1693	42·8	67	2·4	1513	30·2	4524	51·9
Total	2358		2686		3130		3740		3955		2813		4999		8725	

indicated that the stock market has a significant influence on economic life in the United Kingdom.

Table 1.3 gives statistics relating to the type of shareholder investing in U.K. equities. Whilst the market value of private individual investors has grown, their relative importance, percentage wise, has fallen. The real growth has come from the institutional investors who invest the savings of millions of private individuals. The growth in institutional investment has come about as more and more private individuals begin to save, and this is done via insurance companies, pension funds and unit trusts. These institutions have in turn been willing to invest in equities because they have confidence in the workings of the stock exchange, and, of course, because they believe the returns from investing in private enterprise will be adequate to compensate for the risks borne (they assume that society is prepared to continue to accept a capitalist economy).

RETURNS FROM ORDINARY SHARE INVESTMENT

Investment in ordinary shares whilst being more risky offers greater returns than those obtained from fixed interest stocks. A number of studies have been carried out by researchers to measure these returns. The major study in the United Kingdom was undertaken by Merrett and Sykes.[2] They found that the average annual rate of return, compounded annually, for equities in the period 1919 to 1966 came to 9·7 per cent, net of taxes. In estimating this figure they used the De Zoete and Gorton index, an index of stocks of major companies, as a surrogate for equities. This figure of 9·7 per cent compares with an average annual return on consols (U.K. Government Stocks, redeemable at their wish) of 2·3 per cent. Table 1.4 shows the Merrett and Sykes results categorised into three periods. The results clearly show the attraction of equity investment – they offer far higher returns than fixed-interest stocks, and for much of the period since the First World War they have matched and beaten the rate of inflation. However, the returns on ordinary shares are highly volatile, sometimes showing enormous gains and sometimes enormous losses – the impact of this is not shown in Table 1.4. Thus whilst the average annual gain was shown to be 9·7 per cent, investors can, and many have, made large investment losses by buying in bull markets and selling in bear markets. To emphasise the point, Figure 1.1 shows the performance of the

Table 1.3

Institutional equity holdings in U.K.-registered and managed companies

(£m.) 31 December	1966	1967	1968	1969	1970	1971
Insurance companies	2600(11·7)	3366(11·8)	5313(12·9)	4724(13·6)	4595(14·1)	6885(15·1)
Private pension funds	1452(6·6)	1920(6·7)	2850(6·9)	2417(7·0)	2341(7·2)	3416(7·5)
Public pension funds	421(1·9)	602(2·1)	893(2·2)	828(2·4)	917(2·8)	1484(3·3)
Local-authority pension funds	208(0·9)	291(1·0)	485(1·2)	438(1·3)	431(1·3)	754(1·7)
Investment trusts	1625(7·3)	2156(7·6)	3158(7·6)	2671(7·7)	2462(7·6)	3547(7·8)
Unit trusts	453(2·1)	664(2·3)	1142(2·8)	1095(3·2)	1034(3·2)	1635(3·6)
Others	15390(69·5)	19555(68·5)	27360(66·4)	22441(64·8)	20718(63·8)	27796(61·0)
	22149(100·0)	28554(100·0)	41201(100·0)	34614(100·0)	32498(100·0)	45517(100·0)
Combined pension funds	2081(9·4)	2813(9·8)	4228(10·3)	3683(10·7)	3689(11·2)	5654(12·4)
Combined institutions	6759(30·5)	8999(31·5)	13841(33·6)	12173(35·2)	11780(36·2)	17721(39·0)

Source: R. Dobbins, 'Institutional Shareholders in the Equity Market', *Accounting and Business Research*, no. 17 (Winter 1974).

Table 1.4

Average return of year-to-year investments

		Real terms* (%)	Money terms (%)
Pre-war	1919–39	12·4	10·3
War	1939–49	0·3	5·9
Post-war	1949–66	7·4	11·2
Whole period	1919–66	8·0	9·7

* Money terms adjusted for the changing value of money.

Financial Times Ordinary Share Index and the *Financial Times* Actuaries All Share Index since 1962. The volatile nature of these two indexes is clearly shown and one can easily imagine how investors can and have lost a lot of money in the stock market. Figure 1.2 shows the percentage quarterly changes in the *Financial Times* Actuaries All Share index. Table 1.5 shows the volatility of the major stock exchanges throughout the world. This gives the percentage differences between the 'highs' and 'lows' in the market indices of the major stock exchanges in the ten years 1963 to 1972. Clearly, all the major stock markets are fairly volatile and thus provide risky investments.

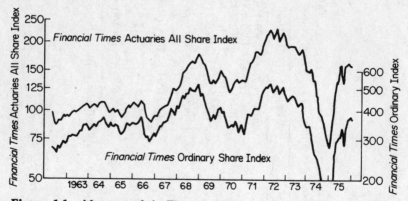

Figure 1.1 *Movement of the* Financial Times *Actuaries All Share Index and the* Financial Times *Ordinary Share Index from May 1962 to December 1975 (log scale)*

Similar studies in the United States have likewise found that the returns on equity shares outstripped those on fixed-interest securities. The major studies here have been carried out by Fisher and Lorie using data from the New York Stock Exchange.[3] The authors

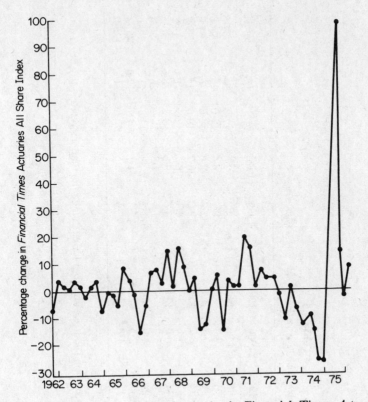

Figure 1.2 *Percentage quarterly changes in the* Financial Times *Actuaries All Share Index*

found that over the entire period 1926–65 the average annual rate of return compounded annually (assuming reinvestment of dividends but ignoring tax) came to 9·3 per cent (an initial equal investment in each stock being made).[4] The results were reported in a set of tables which showed the returns achieved over various periods; Fisher and Lorie also published tables showing the variability of returns.[5]

In an earlier study Cowles found that the annual rate of return, compounded annually, for all stocks quoted on the New York stock exchange in the period 1871 to 1937 came to 6·6 per cent.[6] Although Cowles's methodology differed somewhat from Fisher and Lorie's work, it is doubtful if this had a significant impact on the results. As in the United Kingdom, researchers have found that the annual

Table 1.5

Percentage annual change in national stock market indices

	1963	1964	1965	1966	1967	1968	1969	1970	1971	1972	Ten-year total
United States	19·7	12·8	9·5	−12·6	12·3	10·4	−13·3	−2·5	12·3	14·3	34·5
Canada	10·7	20·7*	1·7	−12·4	9·9	15·0	−0·2	−6·4	12·6	23·1	94·8
United Kingdom	17·6	−9·5	6·7	−7·7	10·8	46·0*	−15·8	−9·8	42·6	0·6	61·6
West Germany	11·1	1·6	−15·7	−18·7	45·9	10·2	19·8	−26·7	19·6	14·6	49·7
France	−16·3	−3·7	−7·0	−11·8	−4·1	9·7	14·4	−8·7	−2·7	20·0	−15·2
Netherlands	14·1	6·0	−11·5	−20·0	33·0	32·7	−8·0	−10·8	−3·2	23·6	48·4
Belgium	13·7	4·1	−6·5	−25·0	16·8	6·6	1·1	1·8*	16·4	26·5	56·6
Italy	−16·1	−29·8	24·4*	4·9*	−6·5	−0·2	11·2	−20·3	−14·8	11·5	−39·6
Australia	22·6*	3·1	11·7	2·5	61·5*	23·8	15·8	−21·1	−4·7	17·8	196·8
Japan	4·4	5·6	15·4	4·8	−8·9	21·3	28·6*	−15·6	48·6*	121·2*	425·6

* Best performing market in each year.

Source: Capital International S.A.: capital international indices, adjusted for exchange fluctuations relative to U.S. dollar.

returns from fixed-interest stocks were far inferior to equities, and the volatility, or riskiness of the returns, was reduced. For a description of two of the major studies on the returns of fixed-interest stocks in the United States see the work done by Weil and Fisher and Weil.[7]

The Pricing Mechanism

Until recently all share deals went through the jobbing system where buyers and sellers of stock purchased and sold to jobbers.[8] Whilst the vast majority of transactions still go through the jobbing system, the introduction of Ariel (Automated Real-Time Investment Exchange Ltd) is obtaining a growing share of institutional business.

The jobbing system involves firms of jobbers who specialise in various types of securities (for example engineering shares or gold shares) and who keep 'books' (i.e. a supply of shares) in these securities. The jobber's function is to buy shares from stockbrokers (acting for their clients – the investors) who want to sell and to sell shares to stockbrokers who want to buy. In order to balance his 'books' the jobber sets the price at which he is willing to buy, and the price at which he is willing to sell, any particular stock. These prices are set so as to give a profit to the jobber, known as the 'jobber's turn', and so as to balance supply and demand. There are usually at least two jobbers who specialise in the leading stocks, and this acts to keep the jobber's turn to a reasonable amount (in view of the financial state of most jobbing firms few would argue that the jobber's turn has been excessive given the riskiness of their business).

The jobbers make prices on the basis of their views of the supply and demand for a particular stock. Thus share prices are set in relation to supply and demand as is the case in a free market. The supply (in the form of investors selling stock – remember share capitals are fixed) and demand functions depend upon a number of factors such as the liquidity requirements of investors, the attraction of alternative investments, and the changing expectations of the returns on various stocks. The latter factor, the changing expectations of future returns by investors, is probably the major reason for supply and demand for a stock. Thus an investor may think that the current 'correct' share price of I.C.I. should be 300p, and if its current market price is, say, 250p, then a purchase is implied and there is a demand for I.C.I. shares by that investor. The investor assumes the I.C.I. share price will rise to 300p in the near future. The process of 'correct' valuing of share prices by investors is known as 'investment analysis'. Share prices are therefore ultimately determined, in large measure, by investment analysis. Investment analysis has developed considerably over the years – not surprising considering the fortunes that can be made and lost on the stock market – and is now a profession in its own right.

THE ROLE OF INVESTMENT ANALYSIS

The formal appraisal of the value of share prices is known as 'investment analysis'. Virtually all institutional investors, for example unit trusts, investment trusts, pension funds, charities, utilise the results of sophisticated investment analysis in their decision-taking. Additionally, even small private investors often make decisions based on a professional's recommendation – this may come from a financial newspaper and these in turn are often derived from a firm of stockbrokers. The institutional investors either employ their own investment analysts or, more likely, utilise the results of stockbrokers' research departments. The work of an investment analyst is to evaluate the worth of a security, to forecast future returns and to build portfolios suitable to the requirements of the investor. Chapters 2 and 3 describe the general methodologies used by practising analysts, with Chapter 2 concentrating on the evaluation of share prices, and Chapter 3 reviewing forecasting of corporate-profits procedures.

Outline of the Book

The aim of the book is to describe the basic methodology of investment analysis and to discuss the implications of this for capital markets.[9] Chapter 2 describes the theoretical valuation of shares and the ways in which analysts attempt to estimate these values, or at least estimate the potential returns. Chapter 3 covers the basic forecasting procedures that are commonly used to forecast corporate profits. The following chapter reviews some of the major studies that have been made into predicting corporate performance from purely statistical measures. Chapter 5 discusses the capital-asset pricing model. This model has received a wide level of adoption as a theoretical explanation of the setting of the level of share prices. The competitive nature of investment analysis and its impact on capital markets are discussed in Chapter 6. This introduces the efficient-markets theory – something which has raised a fair amount of controversy over the years. Chapter 7 reviews the major tests of the efficient-markets theory and discusses some of the problems that have arisen in this research. Chapter 8 discusses some of the recent developments in accounting research that have used an efficient-markets framework. Finally, Chapter 9 presents some concluding remarks and discusses the implications of recent research studies in investments; suggestions for possible future research developments are also given.

CHAPTER 2

The Valuation of Stocks and Shares

The Normative Value of a Share

The normative or theoretical value of a share is the present value of all future receipts that are received in respect of the ownership of that share. The major receipts that come from the ownership of a share are the quarterly, semi-annual or annual dividend and the proceeds from the sale of the share. Thus the theoretical value of a share today, $PVSP$, is expressed thus:

$$PVSP = \frac{D_1}{(1 + r)^1} + \frac{D_2}{(1 + r)^2} + \frac{D_3}{(1 + r)^3} \qquad (2.1)$$

$$\ldots + \frac{D_n}{(1 + r)^n} + \frac{P_n}{(1 + r)^n}$$

where $D_{1, 2, 3, \ldots, n}$ = dividends in each year, P_n = sale proceeds or any terminal receipt (i.e. the liquidation of the company or takeover consideration), and r = discount rate (i.e. the opportunity cost of making the investment or the rate of return required by the investor, taking into consideration the risk involved and the investor's other investment opportunities). This discount rate can vary; for example, the rate may increase through time due to increased risk. For the sake of simplicity the impact of tax has been ignored in equation (2.1).

The theoretical price, usually known as the 'intrinsic value', can now be compared against the existing share price and investment decisions made accordingly. The yield from an investment can also be computed from the above discounting formulae by substituting the current market price (CMP) for $PVSP$ and determining r. Thus:

$$CMP = \frac{D_1}{(1+r)^1} + \frac{D_2}{(1+r)^2} + \frac{D_3}{(1+r)^3} \qquad (2.2)$$

$$\ldots + \frac{D_n}{(1+r)^n} + \frac{P_n}{(1+r)^n}$$

We know CMP, D and P_n and we solve the equation to find r – the yield or annual rate of return.

If the stock market knew with certainty the future cash receipts from owning an investment and knew the discount rate for future

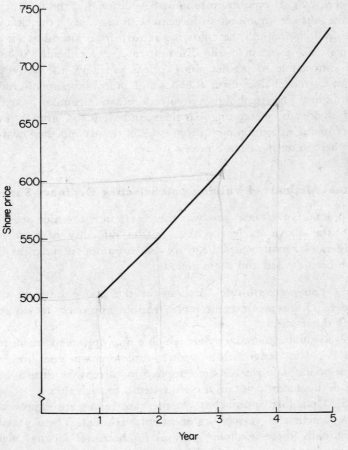

Figure 2.1

periods, then the above theoretical model would almost certainly be in universal use. Share prices would then move in a smooth fashion such as depicted in Figure 2.1; this is a situation where dividends are growing at 10 per cent per annum to infinity and being discounted at 12 per cent.

However, in practice share prices cannot be predicted with accuracy as in Figure 2.1; this can be seen from Figure 1.1, (p. 8) which showed the widely fluctuating movements of the major U.K. stock market indices. The reasons for this are fairly obvious: forecasting dividends into the future is subject to a fair amount of inaccuracy and the forecasting of future share prices (for sale proceeds, P_n) is even more tenuous! Additionally, the future rates of discount are impossible to forecast with certainty – the changing rates of inflation and the changing returns from alternative investments make forecasts of the discount rate very difficult. Although it is impossible to predict share prices precisely, the above discounting model does form the basis of many investment-analysis techniques. These techniques involve forecasting company earnings and dividends, forecasting earnings and dividend growth rates, determining appropriate required rates of return and then evaluating these in terms of share prices.

Actual Methods of Valuing and Selecting Ordinary Shares

In practice investment analysts rarely attempt to value securities with the above model because of the difficulty of forecasting dividends for many years ahead. Instead a number of other methods have been devised and these include:

(1) Using growth-rate forecasts in the above intrinsic value model. This represents the only feasible approach to explicitly using the model.

(2) Evaluating a market yield which is appropriate to the security. This yield is derived from growth-rate forecasts and from risk assumptions. The yield is then applied to current (or future) earnings or dividends to obtain the estimated intrinsic value.

(3) Modelling approaches where share prices are expressed as some function of various independent variables. These variables are usually those involving various fundamental factors such as dividends, earnings and risk.

(4) Determining the future value of the stock market index, probably from various macro factors, and from this estimating individual share prices. As will be seen in Chapter 5, there is some degree of correlation between market movements and individual share price movements (this especially applies in the periods away from the release of fundamental information).

The share prices given by these methods are compared against the existing share prices and investment decisions are made. If the forecast share price is 300p and the actual price is 250p, then a purchase decision is implied. The premise here is that the market price will tend to adjust towards the forecast price in the near future.

In addition to the above methods which arrive at individual share prices, there are methods which indicate purchase or sale decisions without the investor or analyst determining an intrinsic value (i.e. they only know whether a share is under (cheap) or over (dear) valued). The major example, here, is that the analyst compares his opinions of the earnings and asset prospects of the firm against the market's opinions of the firm's prospects. If these differ substantially, then a purchase or sale is implied. This method assumes that (*a*) the stock market uses its forecasts of corporate prospects as a major determinant of share prices, and (*b*) the analyst can forecast the particular firm's prospects better than the stock market, i.e. they have some information on the firm which is not generally known or available, or they can evaluate existing data more accurately. This type of analysis is prevalent when the analyst finds it difficult to interpret the earnings and dividend forecast he has made of the firm into share prices.

In practice analysts tend to use a number of the above methods in making their investment decisions. As an example assume the intrinsic value came to 50p using the discounting approach and that the current price is 30p. Before implementing a buy decision the analyst will probably check

(1) the yield implied by the share price of 50p. Does this seem reasonable?

(2) what earnings, dividends and growth rates are being expected by the market? How do these compare with the analyst's estimates and can the differences be explained?

(3) Is he buying a single share or a portfolio.

Additionally, of course, the analyst will rank various securities by their relative cheapness and purchase accordingly. Up to now we have been considering securities in isolation whereas in point of fact most shares are purchased as a part of a portfolio. The analyst will therefore have to bring portfolio considerations into his analysis when reaching investment decisions. For example, assume two securities, A and B, offered identical expected returns, A's returns being perfectly positively correlated with the market index whilst B's were perfectly negatively correlated with the market index. Whilst the expected returns are the same, most fund managers would go for security B as its addition to the portfolio would result in lower over-all risk than would the addition of share A. The subject of portfolio risk is again briefly referred to on page 26 but otherwise we leave alone the consideration of portfolio aspects.[1]

degrees of future accuracy.

The above methods use fundamental (economic) factors to estimate the intrinsic value. These fundamental factors are usually some combination of earnings, dividends, their growth rates and their past variability. The choice of approach between the various models by individual analysts depends upon the following:

(*a*) The time and expense that analysts and investors can afford, or are prepared, to expend;

(*b*) Analysts' personal opinions as to the accuracy of the methods – past experience and past forecasting accuracy are likely to be the major determinants of an analyst's selection of method;

(*c*) The time period of the forecast. Some methods are more suitable than others for certain forecasting horizons. For example, in short-terms situations (for example where an investor has short-term surplus funds) the forecasting of the market index may be the most appropriate method. This is because away from the release of fundamental information (for example profits' announcements) most securities' prices are strongly correlated with the market index.

There is also another branch of investment analysis known as 'technical analysis'. This attempts to predict share prices on the basis of examining past share price data or other financial data. A brief discussion of technical analysis is given on page 39.

Intrinsic-Value Models

As described earlier, the intrinsic-value model (equation (1.1)) presented at the beginning of the chapter is infeasible because of the number of forecasts required. However, by incorporating growth

$$CMP = \frac{D_1}{(1+r)^1} + \frac{D_2}{(1+r)^2} + \frac{D_n}{(1+r)^n} + \frac{P_n}{(1+r)^n}$$

rates the model becomes tenable. Using growth rates simplifies the calculations involved and allows the forecaster to easily measure the impact of any change in the growth rate or discount rate. The model involves estimating a growth rate (g) at which dividends are expected to grow to infinity (∞) and multiplying the dividend by this figure; thus:

$$V = \frac{D(1+g)}{(1+r)} + \frac{D(1+g)^2}{(1+r)^2} + \frac{D(1+g)^3}{(1+r)^3}$$

$$\cdots + \frac{D(1+g)^\infty}{(1+r)^\infty} \qquad (2.3)$$

$$V = \sum_{t=1}^{\infty} \frac{D(1+g)^t}{(1+r)^t}$$

where V = intrinsic value, D = the dividend just paid, and r = discount rate. In equation (2.3) the dividend in year 1 equals $D(1+g)$, the dividend in year 2 equals $D(1+g)^2$.

The constant growth-rate equation is often shown in a form incorporating continuous compounding of g and r, such that the intrinsic value is the integral

$$V = \int_1^\infty De^{gt}e^{-rt}dt. \qquad (2.4)$$

Thus the intrinsic value is equal to the current dividend D growing at rate g and discounted by rate r over infinitely small time periods dt. This may be integrated to

$$V = \frac{D(1+g)}{r-g}. \qquad (2.5)$$

For the formula to give a solution the discount rate r must be greater than the growth rate g, otherwise the expression would give an infinite answer. This would imply that the firm we are evaluating would eventually control all industry and that we would be prepared to pay an infinite amount for their shares.[2]

All that the model requires is a growth-rate assumption and a discount rate. The growth rate may be estimated from past growth rates of dividends and earnings (although as described on page 68 some researchers have found this simple extrapolation to be spurious when tested on companies) and from some detailed fundamental analysis. This fundamental analysis will probably entail forecasting earnings growth rates and then projecting a dividend growth rate therefrom. Dividends are an appropriation of earnings with earnings being the real measure of a firm's performance.

The level of the discount rate is again somewhat subjective (possible methods are described later on page 24). If the current dividend per share for company A is 20p, the growth rate of the dividend has been estimated at 5 per cent and the required rate of return is 10 per cent, then the value of one ordinary share is

$$V = \frac{20(1 + 0.05)}{0.10 - 0.05}$$
$$V = 420\text{p}.$$

In using the model it is most important that normalised dividends are used (this applies equally so when we use earnings in the model instead of dividends). Thus the dividend in the numerator of the formula should be that paid in a normal year; if the last dividend was abnormally low or abnormally high because of some special factor, then an adjustment should be made. Such abnormality may be present in industries which are subjected to widely fluctuating profitability.

If the analyst feels he can forecast dividends fairly accurately over the next few years, then the model can be adjusted to include the features of equation (2.1) and equation (2.5). Given the following data:

Forecast of dividend per share in year 1   10p
Forecast of dividend per share in year 2   8p
Forecast of dividend per share in year 3   12p
Forecast of dividend per share in year 4   14p
  Forecast growth rate at the end of year 4 =   8 per cent
  Discount rate for years 1, 2, 3 and 4   = 10 per cent
  Discount rate for year 5, r^*, and beyond = 12 per cent

the intrinsic value (V) of the share price is computed as

$$V = \frac{D_1}{(1 + r)} + \frac{D_2}{(1 + r)^2} + \frac{D_3}{(1 + r)^3} + \frac{D_4}{(1 + r)^4} + \frac{\dfrac{D_4(1 + g)}{(r^* - g)}}{(1 + r)^4}$$

$$V = \frac{10}{(1 + 0{\cdot}1)} + \frac{8}{(1 + 0{\cdot}1)^2} + \frac{12}{(1 + 0{\cdot}1)^3} + \frac{14}{(1 + 0{\cdot}1)^4}$$

$$+ \frac{14\,(1 + 0{\cdot}08)/(0{\cdot}12 - 0{\cdot}08)}{(1 + 0{\cdot}1)^4} \qquad (2.6)$$

$$V = 292{\cdot}5\text{p}$$

The formula therefore says that we discount the dividends and the share price at the end of year 4 back to a present value. The share price at the end of year 4 is obtained by implementing equation (2.5) using the year-5 dividend (i.e. $D_4(1 + g)/(r^* - g)$; this is discounted back to today's value, that is divided by $(1 + r)^4$). Again the dividend in year 4 should be 'normalised'.

Another derivation of the model is when an analyst feels he can forecast individual years' dividends and then a growth rate up to a certain horizon. Thereafter the analyst assumes a growth rate which he feels will be achieved by the industry as a whole. This model can therefore incorporate high growth rates for the intermediate term before reverting to an average growth rate to infinity. Assume an analyst can: (1) forecast dividends for each of the three following years; (2) forecast a growth rate g for the following three years (i.e. covering years 4, 5 and 6); and (3) forecast a terminal growth rate of g^*. The intrinsic value model becomes

$$V = \frac{D_1}{(1 + r)} + \frac{D_2}{(1 + r)^2} + \frac{D_3}{(1 + r)^3} + \frac{D_3(1 + g)}{(1 + r)^4} + \frac{D_3(1 + g)^2}{(1 + r)^5}$$

$$+ \frac{D_3(1 + g)^3}{(1 + r)^6} + \frac{D_3(1 + g)^3(1 + g^*)/(r - g^*)}{(1 + r)^6} \qquad (2.7)$$

It is quite simple for additional growth rates to be included in the model although not many analysts go to this length. Each new growth rate is projected on the final dividend at the previous growth rate and the final term is that of equation (2.5) discounted to a present value. Again the dividend to be projected at some growth rate should be normalised. Instead of using the expression $D(1 + g)/(r - g)$ in the intrinsic-value formula, some analysts multiply the final dividend term, i.e. $D_3(1 + g)^3$ in equation (2.7) by a dividend multiple, the product of which is discounted back to today's value (the derivation of appropriate multiples is dealt with later on p. 26).

THE GOLDMAN SACHS MODEL

A model similar to the above in concept has been developed by the American broking firm, Goldman Sachs. The model itself specifies the number of years for which the growth rate *g* is relevant. Beyond this date the growth rate is an average growth rate for a security of that risk class. The time horizon is selected in the following manner. Using historical earnings figures over the past five years and earnings forecasts for as many years ahead as can be obtained from the analyst, a growth trend is computed and extrapolated into the future until the expected deviation of earnings from the trend reaches 7 per cent. The process is repeated adding one more year of historical data (for example 6, 7, 8 and so on) until the growth horizon (the period at which the deviation of earnings reaches 7 per cent) increases no more. This becomes the period over which the firm's specific growth rate is expected to last. The terminal value at the horizon date is given by the computed price–earnings ratio (*PER*). This is assumed to be constant over all firms with (subjectively appraised) similar long-term growth prospects and similar levels of risk. The price–earnings ratio (*PER*) and the rate of return required for the group of similar-type stocks are derived from regression analysis. The theoretical *PER* is compared against the actual *PER* and investment decisions made accordingly.

The published results from using the model for evaluating utilities (for example electricity supply, telephone companies) have shown it to improve returns over those generated from a naive buy and hold policy (i.e. the market index). Unfortunately there have been no recent reports on the predictive ability of the model.

DISCOUNTING EARNINGS

Some analysts prefer to include earnings in the numerator of the present-value formulae, and if they manage to achieve more accurate share price forecasts, then this will certainly be worth while. Amongst the reasons for using earnings are the following:

(1) Earnings have to be projected in any case in order to forecast dividends – dividends being an appropriation of earnings;

(2) Some companies who are expanding quickly or who have temporary liquidity problems may not be paying dividends or may keep their dividends low and thus any projection of these 'abnormal' figures would result in spurious intrinsic values;

(3) Dividends tend to rise in steps and the analyst may find these difficult to forecast as they require not only forecasts of earnings but also of managerial attitudes to dividends.

The earnings used in the intrinsic-value model are multiplied by the pay-out ratio, this of course giving an estimated dividend. The pay-out ratio is likely to be some function of historical pay-out ratios plus subjective judgement as to any changes required. If the earnings per share for the next four years are forecast as 15p, 18p, 20p, 24p and the pay-out ratio is set at 0·4 (i.e. 40 per cent of earnings are paid out as dividends), then the intrinsic-value model is represented thus:

$$V = \frac{15 \times 0\cdot4}{(1 + r)} + \frac{18 \times 0\cdot4}{(1 + r)^2} + \frac{20 \times 0\cdot4}{(1 + r)^3} + \frac{24 \times 0\cdot4}{(1 + r)^4}$$
$$+ \frac{24 \times (1 + g) \times 0\cdot4/(r - g)}{(1 + r)^4} \qquad (2.8)$$

If the analyst does not multiply the earnings per share figure by the pay-out ratio, then some other adjustment will probably have to be made. In times of rapid inflation, historical cost accounting earnings figures do not represent funds which are available for prudent distribution or for net new investment; much of the earnings are required to replace assets which, whilst costing much more than the originals, do not lead to any increase in profitability.

INTRINSIC-VALUE METHODS IN PRACTICE

In practice the intrinsic-value approach has received its widest adoption in the analysis of property and mining companies. This is because analysts have felt themselves able to make more confident predictions about their long-term forecasts and growth rates than for other types of companies. The intrinsic-value approach is also amenable to probabilistic forecasting and sensitivity testing. Here varying forecasts (with their probabilities of occurrence) and assumptions about dividends, earnings, growth rates and discount rates can be made. This will result in ranges of prices within which the share's intrinsic price lies and will tell the analyst of the impact on the intrinsic value for any change in the dividends, earnings or growth rates. The intrinsic-value method can also be used to help evaluate or provide a check on share price forecasts produced by other methods. For example, equation (2.5) can be rearranged to $r = (D/V) + g$ (where D = forecast dividend in current year). If we substitute the predicted share price into V, and as we can forecast D, the coming dividend, fairly easily, and r, the required rate of return, we can compute g. The analyst can then see whether this rate of growth appears to be feasible. Thus, if, say, the modelling approach to share price prediction has produced a forecast of 500p and the required rate of return is 12 per cent and the coming year's dividend is forecast as 10p, then the assumed rate of growth is

$$0 \cdot 12 = \frac{10}{500} + g$$

$$g = 0 \cdot 10$$

$$g = 10 \text{ per cent}$$

Thus the rate of growth assumed by the model (this is probably implicitly assumed) is 10 per cent. The analyst can now see whether this seems feasible taking into consideration his knowledge of the firm.

DISCOUNT RATE

The discount rate used in the intrinsic-value models consists of an amount equal to the time value of money and a premium for the risk borne. Thus the more risky the investment, the greater the risk premium that the investor will require. Although cases have been made out for keeping separate the time-value rate and the risk premium, for all practical purposes they are grouped together; it is, however, worth while for the analyst to explicitly state the risk premium he has applied to the security. The time value of money component is usually taken as being equivalent to the risk-free interest rate such as those on Government securities (this rate differs very slightly between different Government securities, however).

Instead of adding a risk premium to the discount rate, other risk adjustments can be made. One is to multiply the numerators (dividends or earnings) by what is known as 'certainty equivalents'.

These express uncertain future dividends and earnings as certainties – the method involves an investor or analyst specifying his utility function of uncertain future sums.[3] Another method of accounting for risk is to produce probabilistic forecasts. From this a complete pattern of possible outcomes is produced and the investor can make his decisions in the light of these. Probabilistic forecasting is briefly dealt with in Chapter 3. Neither of these methods has achieved much popularity in the United Kingdom so far and so most analysts use a risk-adjusted discount rate.

The assessment of a risk premium is often handled in a fairly subjective manner by investors and analysts. One of the main methods is to estimate the risk premium on the average equity investment on the stock exchange. This figure, together with a subjective adjustment to allow for the specific characteristics of the firm involved, is used as the risk premium for the security. The assessment of the average expected return on equity investment (note this includes both the risk premium and the risk-free rate) can be taken as the average rate of return earned by investors from dividends and share price movements over some period of time. As described in Chapter 1, the average annual rate of return, compounded annually, in the United Kingdom has been found to be 9·7 per cent and in the United States to be 9·3 per cent. The assumption here is that investors are expecting the level of past returns to continue; it also implies that investors have, over the period used in determining the rate of return, been successful in predicting share prices! The analyst should of course adjust the past rate to take account of the following:

(*a*) Any over-all changes in expectations – for example, in the early 1970s most investors would be expecting higher rates of return than existed in the past because of the high rate of inflation and high risk-free interest rates.

(*b*) Any changes in the expected variability of returns;

(*c*) Any changes expected in the long-term economic situation which may affect private enterprise; and

(*d*) Specific characteristics of the industry within which the company operates and any specific considerations of the individual firm itself – for example, instead of using the past rate of returns on equities as a whole, the historical returns on the individual security could be used.

Although the subjective risk premium allocated to a particular share will depend partly on its historical predictability, a major determinant of the risk premium will be the security's portfolio risk characteristics. As most investors hold portfolios of several shares, they will be interested in not only the additional returns generated by a 'prospective' security but also on the change in the riskiness of the portfolio. A share which on its own is quite volatile but which tends to rise when the market falls and vice versa is likely to be attractive to an investor as it reduces portfolio risk. This will probably lead investors to give the share a smaller risk premium and thus a higher market rating. As an approximate guide shares whose values vary very little with the market index are likely to have low portfolio risk.

Market Yields and Multipliers

Many investors and analysts value securities by estimating an appropriate yield or multiplier for the security. The two main statistics used are the dividend yield and the price–earnings ratio multiplier – the latter has been the most popular over the recent past. The dividend yield is given by the following expression:

$$DY = \frac{\text{Dividend per share}}{\text{Share price}}. \qquad (2.9)$$

If an investor decides that an appropriate yield for a particular share is, say, 5 per cent and the current annual dividend is 10p per share, then this implies that the security is worth 200p ($0\cdot05 = 10/$ intrinsic value). If this value is above the current share price, it implies a purchase.

The price–earnings ratio is given by the expression:[4]

$$PER = \frac{\text{Share price}}{\text{Earnings per share}}. \qquad (2.10)$$

If an investor thinks the appropriate *PER* for a particular security is 22 and the earnings per share figure in the last or current year is 15p, then this implies an intrinsic value given by

$$22 = \frac{\text{Intrinsic value}}{15\text{p}}; \text{ that is } 330\text{p}.$$

Again, the value of 330p is measured against the actual share price and investment decisions made accordingly.

The use of dividend yields and price–earnings ratios can also be used in the intrinsic-value models. Thus in the final term of the right-hand side of equation (2.7) we could calculate the terminal value by a yield or multiplier instead of using $D(1 + g)/(r - g)$. However, the main use of yields and multipliers is as described above. Here the last dividend or earnings, or the current year's forecast of dividends, or earnings, are put into the relevant formula (equations (2.9) and (2.10)) along with the estimated appropriate dividend yield or price–earnings ratio. From this the intrinsic values are produced. As mentioned previously, the dividend or earnings figure used should be normalised; if not then some adjustment should be made.

The major difficulty for the analyst is to derive an appropriate price–earnings ratio (or dividend yield; from now on references will be to the *PER* only – this being the method in general use). In practice the assessment of an appropriate *PER* is a subjective one based on an analyst's descriptive evaluation of various fundamental factors and so it is difficult to describe the common methods in use. The factors considered, however, typically include the past performance and future projections of earnings and dividends, historical share price and price–earnings ratio performance and their volatility, managerial ability and the yields from alternative forms of investment. For a personal view of the derivation of *PER*s Cohen and Zinbarg have said:

> The tentative findings of this research suggest that a company's price–earnings ratio has tended during recent years to be higher or lower than the price–earnings ratio of 'the averages' under the following conditions:
>
> 1. P/e is about one point higher (or lower) than the averages for every 1% by which a company's expected five-year growth of earnings power exceeds (or falls short of) the corresponding expected growth of the averages.
>
> 2. P/e is about three fourths of a point higher (or lower) for every 10% by which a company's normal dividend payout ratio exceeds (or falls short of) the payout ratio of the averages.
>
> 3. P/e is one to two points higher (or lower) if a company's sales stability is substantially higher (or lower) than average.

(The average mean absolute percentage deviation of sales from a 10-year trend line is about 5%. The higher the percentage for any given company, of course, the lower its indicated stability.)

4. Price–earnings ratio seems to rise if a large number of financial institutions own a stock – perhaps one point of extra p/e for every 400 institutional owners. The number of institutions owning a stock probably reflects some potpourri of factors that we can lump together under the general heading 'quality'. These factors may include size, nature of trading market, depth of management, product reputation, etc. Data gathered from Standard & Poor's Stock Guide indicate that the average number of institutional owners of the 425 companies included in the S & P Industrials is about 100.

5. Price–earnings ratio tends to vary inversely with financial leverage, other things held constant. P/e is one to two points lower (or higher) than average if a company's financial leverage is substantially higher (or lower) than the average 20% ratio of long-term debt plus preferred stock to total book value of capital.[5]

The major determinants of *PER*s are the growth rate in earnings and the risk factor. The higher the expected growth and the lower the risk, the greater the price–earnings ratio should be. Thus the analyses which go into determining growth rates and discount rates for the intrinsic-value models should also be used in deriving suitable price–earnings ratios. Some analysts have derived growth-rate tables which indicate the growth rates implied by various price–earnings ratios – these tables may for example show earnings growing at a certain rate for a number of years and then growing at some other rate to infinity.[6]

Another method of using price–earnings ratios is to rank them relative to other *PER*s. This method does not set an absolute level for the *PER* but instead ranks it against its past *PER* levels or against an industry or market average. The premise here is that the price–earnings ratio is expected to maintain some sort of relationship over periods of time with either its past values or with the market index. Thus if a security's *PER* has over the past few years averaged 1·2 times that of the market average, then the analyst may, as a first approximation, assume this relationship will continue. Therefore the *PER* is monitored to see if it varies significantly from being 1·2 times the market average; if it does then the analyst should see if he can reconcile the deviation with the fundamental information available, and, if not, then a buy or sell decision is suggested. The relative ranking of *PER*s tends to be a mechanical exercise, and as such it is perhaps more a part of technical analysis than, say, fundamental analysis.

Whilst the analysis that goes into the derivation of *PER*s is usually far less than that which goes into intrinsic-value methods, price–earnings ratio analysis does allow quicker evaluations of shares which may be valuable to the portfolio manager who has a lot of securities to look at. Additionally, *PER* analysis is used as a check against the share prices predicted by other methods.

Regression Models

Another stock-selection methodology that has been used is that of building a causal model which 'explains' the share price. What this means is that the analyst identifies the factors (known as 'independent variables') which influence the share price and then ascertains the relationship between the factor and the share price. Having established a good explanatory model, the analyst now uses the model to predict future share prices and thus the intrinsic value. Typical influencing factors which are incorporated in regression models include historical earnings and dividend rates, forecasts of future earnings and dividend growth rates, the past variability of earnings and dividend rates, and a measure of risk – perhaps the past variability of the share price. Thus the models may include not only known variables but also estimates, i.e. forecasts of future earnings and dividend growth rates. The analyst should of course use his judgement in deciding whether any other variables could be included; for example, in building models for explaining and predicting property share prices, the analyst could include a variable relating to the rate of increase in the asset value per share. Other variables might include variability of earnings and dividends, size, and qualitative factors such as managerial ability. In some cases the analyst may think of a non-obvious variable which may help improve the model. For example, some variables may be associated with the independent variable even though no cause-and-effect relationship can be established. If the inclusion of the variable improves the predictive ability of the model, then it should be incorporated. The analyst will also have to decide what variable to forecast (known as the 'dependent variable'). This will normally be the dividend or earnings yield or the price–earnings ratio; it is only possible to use share prices as the dependent variable when an individual model is built for a security and, as explained later, this is often thought to be unsatisfactory.

The model is quantified by regression analysis,[7] which gives the weightings for the individual factors. The regression also gives various statistics telling the analyst of the reliability that can be placed on the individual factors and on the equation as a whole. Once a satisfactory model has been derived the analyst will now try to see if he can use the model to predict share prices with a reasonable degree of accuracy. This will be assessed by testing the model on another set of data and by testing it in the future.

The form of the regression is symbolised as:

$$\text{Theoretical } PER = a + bZ + cY - dX + e. \qquad (2.11)$$

Thus the yield or *PER* of the share is some function of the factors Z, Y and X. Z, Y and X may represent the future earnings growth, the past dividend growth rate and the past variability of share price. The letters a, b, c and d are known as the regression coefficients and these represent the weightings of the individual factors (the coefficient a is a constant term; see page 33 for an example). The negative sign for d shows that it has an inverse relationship with the price–earnings ratio, i.e. a firm will have a lower *PER* for an increased level of variability in past share prices. The e term is the error term, that is the variation in the *PER* which has not been explained by the model. By inserting observations of *PER*s, forecasts of earnings growth rates, past dividend growth rates and historical variability of share prices, and by using the technique of least-squares linear regression, we can compute the value of the regression coefficients, or weightings, a, b, c and d.

The regression also produces statistics which tell us the importance of the individual factors and the degree of explanation of the movements in the *PER* provided by the model. Sometimes the regression may tell us that a particular factor is of no significance in explaining the variation in the *PER* when, on a rational economic basis, there would seem to be a cause-and-effect relationship. This is often due to interdependence, or in statistical terminology multi-collinearity, between the various independent variables – in other words the impact of one variable on the *PER* is already being accounted for by another variable. The common example in share price models is that the forecast growth in earnings is often highly correlated with the forecast growth in dividends – in many regression models one of these (usually the dividend) will be shown to be of no significance, that is its impact being accounted for in the other variable (i.e. earnings).

The weightings for the models can be constructed for individual securities but this is not met with very often in practice; this is because of the costs involved and because of insufficient data. Regression modelling involves taking numerous observations of a variable, and when building an individual security model this can only be obtained from time-series data. As investor preferences and economic conditions change quite rapidly over time, the use of time-series data, over, say, ten years, is unlikely to lead to accurate prediction models. For this reason regression models are usually of the cross-sectional form where the model explains the industry or market average *PER*. The observations of a variable are taken from all firms, or a sample of all firms, in the particular industry or market.

Once the regression stage has been completed, equation (2.11) may look like

$$\text{Theoretical } PER = 12 \cdot 11 + 83 \cdot 2 Z + 16 \cdot 1 Y - 22 \cdot 7 X.$$

$$(2.12)$$

Thus we have a model with various weights; the 'constant' regression coefficient is $12 \cdot 11$. This means that if the values for Z, Y and X are zero (i.e. zero earnings growth expectations, zero past dividend growth and zero historical share price variability), then the *PER* will be $12 \cdot 11$. We can now use the model to predict individual share prices. This is done by inserting in values of Z, Y and X for the individual security. From this a value for the theoretical *PER* is produced. If the theoretical *PER* is above the actual value, then a purchase is implied, this assuming that the actual value will tend towards the theoretical price–earnings ratio. If a security always appears over- or under-valued when using this method, then an adjustment factor to account for this may be included in the model. The parameters to the model will almost certainly change over time and so continual monitoring and revising of the model will have to be undertaken.

The main advantages of share price models are that once they have been constructed they can be used to value hundreds of shares quite quickly, and they are objective, unbiased and consistent. The disadvantages include the fact that the model needs to be constantly revised, that the model is a market-average model and adjustments have to be made for individual stocks, and finally and most importantly the predictive powers of many models have been found to be poor. The following paragraphs describe some of the major attempts at share price modelling which have been publicised. Most of these have been undertaken in the United States.

THE WHITBECK – KISOR MODEL

In 1963 Whitbeck and Kisor published a paper describing a stock-valuation model developed in the trust department of the Bank of New York – this represented the first major publication of a practical model for stock selection.[8] The basic model says that the *PER* depends upon measures of the projected average annual long-term growth rate in earnings per share, the dividend pay-out ratio and the standard deviation of earnings about a trend (this was used as a surrogate for risk). The price–earnings ratio used was that which related price to 'normalised' earnings. Thus adjustments were made if the firm was at an earnings peak or earnings trough; this usually involved taking an average of several years' earnings. The economic rationale of the model was that investors desire high levels of earnings growth, a high pay-out ratio and low variability in past earnings growth. The model was quantified by taking observations from 135 stocks on 8 June 1962. The expected earnings growth rates were forecasted by the Bank's analysts. The regression produced the following model: theoretical *PER* = 8·2 + 1·5 (earnings growth rate %) + 6·7 (dividend pay-out ratio) − 0·2 (standard deviation of earnings about a trend %).

Thus the model says that, on average, investors were prepared in June 1962 to increase the *PER* by 1·5 points (for example an increase in the *PER* from say 17·0 to 18·5) for every 1 per cent increase in the forecasted earnings growth rate, increase the *PER* by 0·067 points for each percentage rise in the dividend pay-out (i.e. 6·7 × 0·01) and decrease the *PER* by 0·2 points for each unit of standard deviation in the past growth rate (we would expect the risk factor to have a negative sign). The constant of 8·2 shows that the *PER* is 8·2 when the other factors are zero (i.e. zero earnings growth, zero pay-out ratio, zero variability in past earnings growth). Whitbeck and Kisor then used their model to predict the theoretical *PER*s of individual stocks. One example they described was that of I.B.M. They calculated the ratio as

$$PER \text{ of I.B.M.} = 8\cdot2 + 1\cdot5(17\cdot0) + 6\cdot7(0\cdot25) - 0\cdot2(5\cdot0) = 34\cdot4$$

which was very close to the actual *PER* of I.B.M. when using normalised earnings. This implied that I.B.M. was correctly valued at that time.

Whitbeck and Kisor tested their model on four different valuation dates (i.e. they revised the regression coefficients at these dates to incorporate up-to-date forecasts) and observed the performance of the stocks in the three months succeeding each valuation date. They found that stocks whose actual *PER* was below 85 per cent of the theoretical outperformed the market average (in the succeeding three months) and that stocks whose actual *PER* was greater than 115 per cent of the theoretical *PER* underperformed the market average; in between 85 per cent and 115 per cent the predictive ability appeared weak. Unfortunately there has been little further testing of the model to see how relevant it is today.

BOWER AND BOWER

Another attempt at share price model-building was made by Bower and Bower.[9] They derived the following relationship over the four years 1960–4:

$$\log PER = 3\cdot14 + 0\cdot847 \log(1 + G) + 0\cdot095 \log(PAY)$$
$$+ 0\cdot080 \log(MKT) - 0\cdot077 \log(CON) + 0\cdot534 \log(VAR)$$
$$+ 0\cdot976 \log(FIR),$$

where $\log PER$ = logarithm of the price–earnings ratio using normalised earnings, G = growth rate in earnings, PAY = dividend pay-out rate, MKT = market capitalisation of the ordinary stock of the company, CON = a coefficient relating the change in the rate of return to the firm's stockholder with the change in the rate of return on the Dow Jones Industrial Index (a market index) – the negative sign was expected, i.e. that investors are averse to risk, VAR = the difference between the stock's high and low price in a year as a fraction of the stock's average price – surprisingly the sign was positive but the Bowers suggested a plausible explanation for this, *FIR* = the difference between the actual *PER* and a theoretical *PER* given by the above model (with the variable *FIR* omitted of course) – this variable is therefore said to represent all the remaining factors influencing the price–earnings ratio.

The Bowers' model used historical data only and so is a form of mechanical trading rule. If this had been found to be successful, then the model would be used by everyone and thus discounted away. The authors tested the model on 100 stocks over the period 1960–4 but found it was of little predictive value – although a good explanatory fit was found, the model proved to be of little use in accurately forecasting future share prices.

AHLERS'S MODEL

Ahlers's model is basically similar to the Whitbeck and Kisor model previously described but the actual make up of the variables is changed.[10] The model is of the form:

$$\log PER = a + b \log[(R_i/SE_i) + 1] + c \log(YD_i/AP_i) - d \log(CVAR_i),$$

where R_i/SE_i is the growth rate in normalised earnings for security i – these are estimated by the analyst (Ahlers's article explains the process by which the growth rates are calculated), YD_i/AP_i = current dividend yield on security i, $CVAR_i$ = the coefficient of variation associated with the earnings forecast – the sign of this variable was negative as expected.

The model allows the analyst to monitor the accuracy of his forecasting, thus helping improve future predictions.

Ahlers tested the model for 1964 using twenty-four randomly selected stocks. The regression equation was constructed using quarterly data from the beginning of 1958. The results showed that stocks which were considered undervalued by the model subsequently outperformed the market index (the Standard & Poor's '425' was used), whilst those stocks which were considered overvalued by the model underperformed the market index. Ahlers concluded that the model's success rate in predicting undervalued stocks was far higher than the success rate of analysts and it also outperformed the market average.

WEAVER AND HALL

Weaver and Hall published a paper in 1967 which reported a share price model used by their firm – a major British stockbroker.[11] The form of the model was as follows:

$$\log y = a_0 + a_1 \log x_1 + a_2 \log x_2 \ldots + a_5 \log x_5,$$

where y = mean dividend yield, x_1 = mean pay-out ratio, x_2 = the forecast short-term earnings growth rate, x_3 = the forecast long-term dividend growth rate, x_4 = the historical earnings variability, x_5 = historical earnings growth rate.

The coefficients for earnings and dividends growth rates (x_2, x_3 and x_5) were found to be negative, this being as expected. Again, the regression coefficients were derived from a cross-sectional analysis of companies and the coefficients were then used to calculate individual company theoretical dividend yields and hence share prices. Weaver and Hall tested the model against buy and hold strategies and found that the model approach achieved superior results. Since their paper in 1967 the variables of the model used by Weaver and Hall's firm have undergone various changes – the model approach is still being used but in conjunction with the individual analyst's appraisals.

OTHER MODELS

Other models which have received a fair amount of attention include the following:

(1) *Gordon's model*.[12] This incorporated six variables, being dividends per share, expected growth in dividends, a measure of earnings' stability, a measure of the firm's capital gearing or leverage, an index of operating asset liquidity, and a measure of the firm's size.

(2) *Benishay's model*.[13] This included an earnings growth rate, a growth rate in share price, a pay-out ratio, the variability of earnings, variability of share price, market capitalisation, and a debt–equity ratio, in the model.

(3) *Lerner and Carleton's model*.[14] The independent variables in this model are investor and corporate expectations of the pay-out ratio, rate of return, asset figure, risk-free interest rate, the income-tax rate, the debt–equity ratio and a risk measurement.

As can be seen from the models briefly reviewed above, earnings and dividends expectations are very common factors; the variability in past earnings is also a popular independent variable.

SUMMARY OF REGRESSION MODELS

Whilst most of the models which have used purely historical data have yielded high degrees of explanatory significance (given by the R^2 statistic – the coefficient of determination) when explaining past share prices, there appears to be no way in which they can success-fully predict future prices. These models are examples of mechanical investment rules described on page 42. Once these models have been widely publicised one would expect their profitability to be dis-counted away by rational investors.

The only regression models which have reported successful prediction of share prices are those which incorporate forecasts of future earnings, dividends and their growth rates – and the con-tinuing success of the models appears to hinge largely on the accur-acy of the forecasts. These models are not mechanical rules as they require forecasts of future earnings, and so on, and so use basic fundamental analysis. Unfortunately there has been little research into the continuing predictive ability of these models.[15] The major practical requirements for modelling are to continually reappraise the regression coefficients as these are likely to change over time and, most important of all, to obtain accurate forecasts of the inputs into the model. As a final point it is worth noting that if an analyst had been able to derive a very successful model, then he would be unlikely to publicise it, and thus there would be no record of its existence and its success (the analyst would presumably be working entirely on his own account).

Predicting the Market Index

Many shares have been found to have 'relatively' stable relation-ships (see Chapter 5) to the market index and this has provided analysts with yet another stock-selection technique. There are two main ways in which the market index method is used:

(1) Examining whether the current share price is being valued according to its historical relationship with the market index. For example, a stock's relationship may show its price to move 1·2 times as fast as the market index. Thus if the market index has risen by

100 per cent in a period, we would expect the share price to have risen 120 per cent. If, however, the share price has only risen by 80 per cent, then this may imply that the share is undervalued – i.e. it has temporarily got out of line with the market index. Before committing himself to a purchase decision the investor should see if there are any significantly changed fundamental factors which may have accounted for the discrepancy.

(2) If we have a forecast of the future level of the stock market, then we can predict individual share prices associated with this market level. The major difficulty in this analysis is predicting the level of the stock market: another difficulty is that a share's historical relationship with the stock market, whilst being reasonably stable, is not fool-proof (as Chapter 7 will explain, the R^2, or degree of variation in the share price explained by the market index, is only of the order of 0·2 or 0·3 for the majority of stocks).

Many researchers have attempted to discover influences on the stock-market index. The most common factors cited are corporate profitability, money supply, growth in the economy and movements in the returns from alternative investments. Figure 2.2 shows the

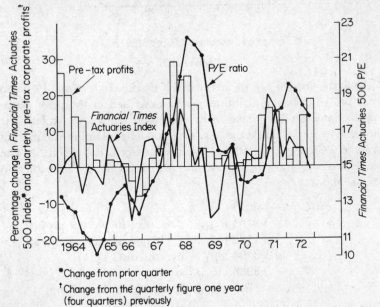

*Change from prior quarter
†Change from the quarterly figure one year
(four quarters) previously

Figure 2.2   *The relationship between the* Financial Times *Actuaries 500 Index and quarterly pre-tax corporate profits*

movements in corporate profits and the *Financial Times* Actuaries
500 Index. Clearly, there is a close correlation between the
two – unfortunately for analysts the stock market appears to lead
the disclosure of company profits. Whilst this is evidence that the
stock market is accurately discounting future earnings, it also
means there is no easy way to forecast the market index (i.e. from
reported earnings). Figure 2.3 shows a similar experience in the
United States.

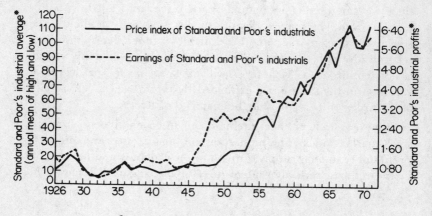

*Based on Standard and Poor's '425' stocks

Figure 2.3

Analysts who do try to forecast the market index usually do so
from basic fundamental influences as described in the prior para-
graph. Some analysts have built regression models to explain the
movements in the market index. One model explaining the market
average *PER* for U.K. stocks has been described by Hall.[16] The
model derived and the regression coefficients appropriate thereto
are as follows:

$$\log_{10} PER = -9.5519$$
$$+ 1.8153 \log_{10} (\% \text{ change in pre-tax profits})$$
$$+ 3.1192 \log_{10} (\% \text{ change in excess money})$$
$$+ 1.3294 \log_{10} (\text{investment/G.D.P.})$$
$$- 0.8988 \log_{10} (\text{cover})$$
$$- 0.1726 \log_{10} (\% \text{ change in Bank Rate})$$

Percentage explained   = 97 per cent
Standard error of equation = 4 per cent

The derivation of the independent variables is explained in Hall's paper and this should be referred to by the interested reader. The percentage change in pre-tax profits relates to the change in quarterly profits from those four quarters (one year) earlier.

The model provided a good explanation of the actual movement in the *PER* of the *Financial Times* Actuaries 500 Index: the percentage of variance in the market *PER* index explained was 97 per cent. Its use as a medium-term forecasting device is much more tenuous, however.

Technical Analysis

Technical analysis is the name given to forecasting techniques which utilise historical data only, many of which have no fundamental economic logic. Past share prices prove to be the major data source used by technical analysts although other statistics such as volume of trading and stock market indices are also utilised. The technical analyst looks at the past data to see if he can establish any patterns or relationships. He then looks at the current data to see if any of the established patterns are applicable and, if so, extrapolations can be made. The rationale behind technical analysis is that share price behaviour (or other financial data) repeats itself over time and the analyst attempts to derive methods to predict this repetition. Share prices are determined by the demand–supply relationship, and the 'intrinsic value' is but one factor in this complex function. A multitude of other influences come into play but they are very difficult to quantify on their own. The combined impact of these factors are, however, reflected in share prices. The protagonists of technical analysis claim that it is only by examining past share price behaviour that future share prices can be accurately predicted. As will be described later in Chapter 7, the efficient-markets theory contends that technical analysis does not have any successful predictive ability. However, many analysts engage in technical analysis and many investment decisions are made on the basis of it.

Technical analysis is generally used as a short-term forecasting technique; sometimes it is used for timing the purchase of a share which is already deemed desirable to hold. Additionally, it is sometimes used in conjunction with other methods, i.e. a 'buy signal' may be required from both the intrinsic-value formula and the technical-analysis rule for a purchasing decision to be made.

Some rules devised by analysts give explicit share price levels whilst others just give buy or sell signals without any firm indication of the increases or decreases to be expected. It is up to the individual analyst how much reliance he places on the results – this will be gained from experience. Many technical analysts say that their methods are not fool-proof but that they work more often than not and are therefore profitable – this especially applies to those advocating various mechanical investment rules.

To some extent technical rules can be self-fulfilling in that if a pattern appears which suggests a certain future price performance, and if sufficient analysts believe in the pattern, then they will all make the same purchase or sell action and continue until the price is pushed to the theoretical level. Thus any pattern which is widely believed in will be self-fulfilling to some extent. This will result in analysts attempting to predict patterns at earlier and earlier stages such that the pattern may not be formed in the way envisaged. This process of competing analysts driving away profit potential from technical patterns helps create an efficient market (see Chapter 6 for a discussion of efficient markets).

Technical analysis is traditionally divided into two categories, one being the use of charts, the other being various mechanical investment rules. Chart analysis is based upon recording past share price observations on a chart, reading some sort of pattern into it and extrapolating from it so as to reach a forecast.

The first thing an analyst will do is to build up a chart showing the share price behaviour. Various scales can be adopted, two of the major ones being bar charts (showing the share price for each day or other period) and point and figure charts (which record successive price increases and successive price decreases in individual columns; each time there is a price reversal – a move in the opposite direction – a move is made to a new column). Having built up the chart the analyst now has to interpret it to see if any particular pattern appears to be forming. There are certain standard patterns that are said to occur fairly frequently. Common patterns include those with descriptive terms such as 'congestion areas', 'trends' and 'channels', 'triangles' and 'head and shoulders' patterns. Figure 2.4 shows an example of a point and figure chart for European Ferries.[17] A head and shoulders pattern has been established and these are marked on the figure (*A, B, C, D*) together with a 'neckline' which is drawn across the bottom of the shoulders.

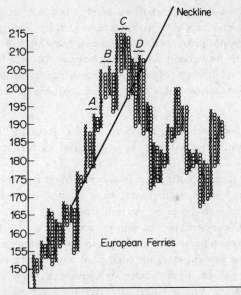

Figure 2.4 *'Head and shoulders' pattern: an example*

The next step the analyst has to make is to determine the future movement of the pattern – clearly a most important step! This requires considerable subjective judgement on the part of the analyst – most analysts given the same chart would interpret it slightly differently from each other and their forecasts based on the chart may differ significantly (some suggesting a purchase, some suggesting a sale). It must be emphasised that forecasting from charts is a very personal art and there are no strong guidelines which can be set out. The choice of the type of chart to use and the choice of scale can lead to varying patterns appearing – again the choice is very much personal preference.

The second category of technical analysis are mechanical investment strategies. Instead of plotting share prices on charts they and other financial data are arranged into arithmetical formulae and ratios. At certain points the rule will require that action be taken, for example, a purchase or sale. Many of the rules are ranking methods which give relative forecasts and these are often short-term predictions. The rules are based on past data which showed profitable results. Following technical analysts' claims that patterns exist, these mechanical rules which worked on past data

are assumed to work, at least more often than not, on future data.
Unlike charts, the mechanical rules are usually very explicit and
little or no personal judgement is required. For this reason mechanical trading rules have been subject to considerable academic testing
and the results of this type of research are summarised in Chapter 7.

Amongst the major rules which are commonly met are the
following:

(1) *Leading indicators.* This is where various statistics (for example
volume of trading, money supply) lead major turning points in the
stock market;

(2) *Relative strength tests.* This is where investors reallocate their
portfolio at the end of each period so as to be invested in the best
performing stocks of the prior period, this being based on the premise that good performance in one period is likely to be repeated,
more often than not, in the next period – derivations of relative
strength include moving-average formulae where purchase decisions
are implied if a stock moves above its moving average; and

(3) *Formula plans.* This is where the investor has a plan which tells
him how much to invest and when

Although these rules are in common use, each analyst has to
decide what the appropriate action points are for his particular
usage of the rule. Equally the analyst should monitor the success
of the rule and revise the action limits where appropriate (this
revision is likely to be required quite often).

Summary

This chapter has outlined some of the major share-selection techniques in use by practising investment analysts. Many of these
techniques are used in conjunction with one another in making
investment decisions. It should be obvious by now that forecasts of
corporate earnings are an extremely important input into many of the
share-evaluation models. Thus Chapter 3 briefly describes the work
of analysts in forecasting corporate profitability and Chapter 4 looks
at some of the academic-based statistical research into the predictability of earnings.

CHAPTER 3

Forecasting Company Profits

As shown in Figures 2.2 and 2.3, the level of company earnings is highly correlated with the level of the stock market index and thus accurate forecasts of corporate profitability can lead to highly profitable investment selections. This applies to both macro investment, i.e. forecasting the general level of corporate profits and making broad investment decisions relating to equities as a whole, or at the micro level where individual stock selection takes place. Studies in the United States by Latané and Tuttle,[1] and Kisor and Messner[2] have also found that earnings are associated with individual share prices. These studies showed that, on the average, companies whose earnings changed by the greatest amounts also experienced the greatest share price change. As with share prices (see Chapter 5) an individual firm's growth in earnings tends to have some positive correlation with all firms' earnings, and hence predictions of one from the other can be made. Forecasts of corporate earnings and dividends are also required for all the fundamental share-selection models described in Chapter 2. In fact, given very accurate forecasts of earnings and dividends (dividends being a function of earnings) the share-selection models of Chapter 2 will give 'correct' share prices over various time horizons. Therefore the accuracy of the forecasting of corporate earnings is of vital importance in valuing securities and forms the major part of the work-load of investment analysts.

Forecasts can be made for various lengths of periods and the techniques employed may vary as the time horizon lengthens. Obviously, forecasting becomes more tenuous the further ahead the horizon is, but these forecasts may lead to the greatest returns especially for large-scale investors who are unable to switch in and out of large blocks of shares. The forecasting time horizons that are in fairly common use can be categorised as follows:

(*a*) following-year profits plus subsequent growth rates – this is the type of forecasting required for price–earnings ratio share-selection methods;

(*b*) forecasting earnings for the next three or four individual years and then subsequent growth rates.

The actual time horizon of a forecast will depend partially on the requirements of the investor (who, for example, may only be a short-term investor), partially on the degree of accuracy the analyst feels he can achieve. The earnings of some industries such as property investment and mining companies may be easier to forecast over long periods than for other, more volatile and complex industries.

General Methodology

The general methodology of forecasting corporate profits involves breaking down a company's activities into its various parts, breaking down its revenue and cost structure, forecasting the future values of these broken-down constituents of activities, revenues and costs, consolidating the forecasts of the constituents into the whole, and consolidating separate items such as finance charges and taxes. This will give earnings per share forecasts for the various years looked at. The assessment of growth rates will also involve the above methodology although statistical extrapolations of past growth into forecasted future earnings per share figures may be in use as well. The forecasting of the various items making up the costs and revenues often involves utilising leading indicators – leading indicators are statistics which are correlated with, say, a firm's sales but whose values are known in advance (there may be a cause-and-effect relationship or there may be just an association with no cause-and-effect rationale). They are therefore used to forecast future values of the firm's sales. Typical leading indicators include trade and economic statistics which are collected and published at, say, monthly intervals. Analysts also collect items of news which are specific to a company's performance, for example the winning of a major contract, the occurrence of a strike, movements in the price of a basic commodity such as copper which would affect the cost structure of, say, an electrical manufacturing company.

There are many and varied data sources for helping undertake the above basic methodology. In breaking down a firm's activities and its revenue and cost structure the company's annual report and accounts usually forms the initial data base. Thus several years of accounting data are examined so as to get a general idea of the company's performance; this may also help highlight major reasons for the performance. There are several agencies who prepare statistical summaries of the data appearing in annual reports and these give a very concise and convenient summary of the firm's financial history. In forecasting future performance leading indicator statistics prove very useful and these can be found in trade journals and economic journals. Data relating to specific companies can be gained from trade journals, newspapers and from talking to and visiting companies. Analysts should make a point of regularly reading the major journals and perusing other pertinent, although perhaps less relevant, sources. There are a number of economic agencies which also prepare in-depth surveys of industries and these can yield very valuable information.

Apart from the above basic analyses an increasing number of analysts are turning to using quantitative methods such as probabilistic forecasts and simulation; these will be briefly described later. An analyst is also likely to take part in discussions of general economic forecasts. These forecasts will be used as broad parameters to the forecasts by analysts of individual stocks, for example a stockbroking firm would be using consistent economic assumptions for all of its forecasts of U.K. securities. Analysts need to take part in these discussions both because they may well have something to contribute and so as to ensure they are going to use these economic parameters in their individual share evaluations.

The Annual Report and Accounts

The annual report and accounts provide a good deal of basic information to analysts such as the following:

(1) They provide an initial insight into the business' activities and the past financial performance – past performance is an important indicator of the capability of management;

(2) They indicate key areas of profitability and efficiency – the

critical items which have an important bearing on the variability of corporate earnings can be appraised – for example, the impact of financial gearing on earnings per share can be measured;

(3) Time series of accounting data can be measured against various trade and economic indices to help determine reasons for performance and so as to examine the feasibility of using these indices in forecasting future results; and

(4) The accounts provide bases from which projections of past figures and trends can be made.

The major contents of the report and accounts are the following:

(*a*) *A profit and loss account.* This shows the revenues earned and the costs incurred in the particular period (usually one year). It thus gives a financial measure of the company's activities and performance throughout the year. One of the major problems in preparing profit and loss accounts is that many transactions take time to complete (i.e. civil-engineering contracts) and thus the accountant has to estimate how much profit to take. The final figure appearing in the profit and loss account is usually the earnings per share (E.P.S.) figure, this representing the earnings for the year attributable to each share. Part of these earnings are normally distributed as dividends whilst the remainder is invested inside the business providing funds for asset replacement and expansion. The earnings per share figure and its rate of growth form a major yardstick quoted by investors when measuring performance. It is the figure which is multiplied by the price–earnings ratio to obtain an intrinsic value. If the company has subsidiaries, then the profit and loss account has to incorporate their results – it then becomes known as a 'consolidated profit and loss account'.

(*b*) *A balance sheet* and if there are subsidiaries, a consolidated balance sheet. This shows the assets, liabilities and the net worth of the shareholders at one point in time – the year end. The balance sheet sets out these items in a fair amount of detail. The assets are normally valued at cost less depreciation and so the balance sheet does not represent the economic value of the business (i.e. the present value of future income streams) or the current market value (i.e. the value of the company if broken up). Recently there has been a move towards the adoption of inflation-adjusted accounting which results in a more true view of a firm's state of health. Quoted companies are now expected to produce a set of inflation adjusted accounts as a supplement to historical cost accounts although this is not yet a legal requirement. Both the profit and loss account and the balance sheet are reported on by an independent firm of auditors which has to express an opinion as to whether they are in compliance with the *Companies Acts* of 1948 and 1967. The auditor's report gives a certain amount of credence to the annual accounts.

(*c*) *Notes to the accounts.* This gives data which have to be disclosed in the accounts. However, the *Companies Acts* allow data to be presented in the 'notes' and most companies take advantage of this. This is usually because it makes the accounts less cluttered and thus more presentable.

(*d*) *A statement of sources and uses of funds statement* is now being given by many companies following a recommendation made by the senior accounting bodies. This statement shows for the period under review the sources of additional funds and the uses to which they have been applied. Thus it provides information as to how the activities of the enterprise have been financed and how its financial resources have been used during the period covered – it does not, however, purport to show the capital requirements of a business or the extent of seasonal peaks of debtors, creditors, inventories, and so on. It has become an increasingly important analysis as modern methods of financing have become more diverse and complex and the normal form of profit and loss accounts and balance sheets have not given the necessary information.

(*e*) *The Chairman's report.* This usually consists of a descriptive explanation of the year's activities and performance, developments that have occurred during the year and prospects for the forthcoming year.

(*f*) *The Director's report.* This normally gives certain factual information relating to the year under review which has to be disclosed by law.

In addition to the annual accounts the stock exchange requires that quoted companies publish half-yearly financial statements (a few firms go further than this in fact and publish quarterly reports). These statements usually include the firm's profits, sales, earnings per share and dividend per share; again some firms go further and give more detailed information in their half-yearly report. Although these interim statements are usually unaudited, they do provide valuable data to the investment analyst.

For companies who have subsidiaries, accounts of these subsidiaries as well as the consolidated accounts have to be lodged at Companies House. Analysts should examine the subsidiaries' accounts. He should also make sure that the subsidiaries' accounts and those of the parent add up to the consolidated accounts – in companies which have a complicated group structure the analysis can be very complex. The analysis of subsidiaries' accounts can be especially useful as separate subsidiaries are often set up because:

(1) they make specific products;
(2) they serve specific markets;
(3) they depend upon geographical location;
(4) they are under separate management; and
(5) they may represent separate parts of the manufacturing process.

Thus breaking down the accounts by subsidiaries often gives valuable information on revenue and cost structures and the activities of the group.

The individual contents of the above components of the annual report and accounts are governed by the *Companies Acts* of 1948 and 1967, the stock exchange and by the major accounting bodies. Although only the *Companies Acts* have legal sanctions, the other two forces do get acceptance of their recommendations. Specifically, the stock exchange can suspend the quotation of a company if it does not comply with the exchange's requirements and this will result in the loss of marketability of the firm's securities. The major accounting bodies can exert their influence largely through getting their members committed to the profession's official views. (It is in fact the **a**ccounting bodies' recommendations which have been the least well accepted in practice. Many quoted companies have adopted different modes of presentation and different accounting measures than those advocated by the profession.) These bodies have made regulations and recommendations as to minimum amounts of information disclosure that must be given by companies – few companies give much more than the minimum. Apart from the type of information that must be disclosed, rules and guidelines have been laid down which state how and in what form this information should be shown.

Both the *Companies Acts* and the stock exchange have been fairly reticent about the rules and procedures by which the accountant should prepare the accounts. The major influence has been the accountancy profession itself which have evolved 'generally accepted accounting principles' (G.A.A.P.). The major generally accepted conventions and concepts of accounting are the following:[3] the going concern basis, the accruals basis, consistency, prudence and the use of cost as the major measurement of profit-and-loss and balance-sheet items. The last reference, the use of cost, has come under scrutiny lately and, as stated before, companies are now expected to also produce inflation-adjusted profit and loss accounts and balance sheets. This involves adjusting historical cost figures by inflation indices based on replacement costs and general levels of inflation. These generally accepted accounting principles were developed to make accountancy a practical science. However the G.A.A.P.s are not consistent with the economic concepts of income and capital and they have therefore come under attack in academic quarters. Specifically, the economic concept of corporate value has been defined as the discounted stream of future earnings and the economic definition of income as the periodical change in the discounted stream of future earnings.[4] This of course is extremely appropriate for investment analysis – in fact it is this value they are trying to get at and one which is required in share-valuation techniques. In the real world of uncertainty, however, these values will be very tenuous and thus the generally accepted accounting principles have been evolved as the 'best' measures of evaluating income and capital.

Recently the major accounting bodies have set up an accounting standards committee (A.S.C.) with the aim of producing uniform and consistent methods of accounting for economic transactions. The statements of the A.S.C. have to some extent 'codified' G.A.A.P.s as well as looking at more detailed items of current interest. The accounting profession is expected to follow A.S.C. statements of standard accounting practice, although many have not done so. The major advantage of standards on accounting practice is that investors and other outsiders will have a better idea of how various figures have been arrived at, thus allowing sounder interpretation and comparability with other companies. The major argument against detailed, rigorously enforced standards is that individual firms and industries have their own accounting problems, and hence to enforce common standards can lead to misleading financial statements.

Variations in Accounting Practice

Within the generally accepted accounting principles, however, there is considerable scope for individual treatment by companies. Examples include:

(1) Depreciation. Here firms can use whatever rate of depreciation they like and whatever method they like, for example straight-line, reducing balance, sum of the years' digits. Thus two similar-type firms with identical assets may have vastly different depreciation expenses appearing in the profit and loss account. The only requirement that a firm needs to follow is that of consistency. If the method of depreciation changes or the rates of depreciation change and the amounts involved are material, then this should be disclosed in the accounts. Very few companies give information on the rates of depreciation they use and so the analyst must resort to estimating them, and this is very difficult if the firm is diversified in any way. The impact of depreciation is very great in most industrial concerns, although some commercial organisations, for example travel agencies, may have negligible depreciation.

Differences can also arise in asset valuation especially when the values have fallen. Recently many companies with significant property assets have not reduced the value of these even though the market value has dropped substantially. This was partly because the companies argued that they where holding the assets for long-term development and that the current 'depressed' property values were temporary. Even where property values have been reduced this has often thought to be insufficient by the auditors and this has led to a number of auditor's qualifications.

(2) The treatment of research and development costs, goodwill and other intangible assets varies between companies. Some companies may expense these costs in the year they occur, thus reducing profit – if the expenditure has a future value, then the practice will be understating the strength of the business. On the other hand, some firms capitalise all the expenditure and provide little or even no depreciation. Whilst it is generally accepted that the assets do depreciate, the time period over which this is done is entirely at the discretion of the firm (the auditors can make qualifications in their report, however, if they think this is necessary). Whilst the analyst may be aware of these different practices the accounts

rarely describe the precise policy followed. This can make it difficult to make comparisons between firms.

(3) Inventory or stocks, have to be valued at cost (in the historical cost accounts) but in times of varying prices the precise cost of the inventory is rarely known – it being too costly to separate stocks purchased at different prices. In respect of this a number of methods for estimating costs have been derived. These include average cost, first-in–first-out and last-in–first-out. Each of these methods gives different 'costs', and in times of rapidly changing prices and changing physical quantities the alternative methods can give greatly differing earnings and inventory figures.

(4) Long-term contracts. Many firms are in industries such as civil engineering where the main work-load takes several years to complete. In such cases there are several ways in which firms can take profits and thus comparisons between firms become tenuous. Although many firms disclose in their accounts the broad methods of taking profits on long-term contracts, this is rarely detailed enough for the analyst to get a precise idea of the profitability of the contract.

(5) Bad debts and other provisions. Firms have to estimate various provisions they think will be necessary to cover possible losses in the current year but which will not manifest themselves until a following year. Amongst the most common of provisions are those relating to bad debts, sales returns, guarantees and legal costs and settlements in respect of outstanding claims. The accountant has more or less a free hand in how much he decides to provide for, providing it is within reason. Again the auditors can qualify the accounts if they think the provisions are unreasonable (especially if on the low side), but as qualifications are now so common, even for very respectable companies, this is not the constraint it was once thought.

(6) The A.S.C. has recommended that firms show material gains or losses from extraordinary items separately in the profit and loss account. Extraordinary gains or losses are those that arise from transactions which are not a recurrent part of its activities (for example profit or loss on the sale of an asset or losses due to hurricane damage) – the reason for showing them separately is so as to emphasise that they are non-recurrent and thus should not be extrapolated into the future. Although the accounting standard relating to extraordinary items (S.S.A.P. 6 (1974)) was supposed

to be definitive, it has in fact created an alternative place for reporting transactions. Thus there is some discretion available to management in deciding whether a transaction is extraordinary or not, and thus whether it should be reported in the main body of the profit and loss account or in the extraordinary-items section. Additionally, some gains are taken automatically to reserves – this often being the practice when recording increases in property values. It is therefore possible for a transaction to be regarded as extraordinary in one company whereas an identical transaction may be recorded as an everyday expense by another firm. This again provides problems for analysts in evaluating and comparing companies.

(7) Quoted companies are now expected to produce an inflation-adjusted set of accounts and the current cost method has been advocated. Although there is as yet no history of how firms will proceed, it looks as though it will be up to the individual company to evaluate appropriate 'inflation-adjusted' costs. This provides yet another opportunity for managers to adjust the accounts to suit their needs.

(8) Non-physical assets such as goodwill, brand names and the value of the work-force are not usually incorporated in the balance sheet unless purchased. Thus valuable assets of a business are often not recorded in the accounts.

The degree of variety that can be achieved in recording one transaction is quite staggering. Spacek discussed the possibilities in a well-referenced article.[5] Table 3.1, taken from Spacek, gives an example of how the earnings per share for a typical company could be reported as anywhere between $0·80 and $1·79. This relates to just six different methods of reporting the profits of the year. Chambers has gone on record as having said that over one million earnings' figures can be calculated from the same basic data.[6]

In 1967, *Forbes Magazine* published an article entitled 'What Are Earnings? The Growing Credibility Gap' which quoted a number of economic transactions which had been reported differently in the accounts of competing companies in the United States. Amongst the examples quoted were the following:

(1) In 1962 a profit of $80 million on the sale of the Ethyl Corporation was made. Ethyl was jointly owned by General Motors and Standard Oil of New Jersey; General Motors reported the profit in its profit and loss account whilst Standard Oil included

it in its 'Statement of Stockholders' Equity' (i.e. in its balance sheet). General Motors' treatment could be construed by investors to mean that income from its normal operations had increased.

(2) In 1964 Gulf and Western, a large diversified corporation, changed its method of accounting for exploration and development costs and thereby increased its earnings for 1965 and 1966 by $1·6 million.

(3) Sun Oil expenses its drilling costs for oil wells immediately whilst Continental Oil capitalises the costs of successful wells and depreciates them gradually. There are many examples of different treatments of research and development costs and this is an area where the A.S.C. in the United Kingdom are expected to bring in guidelines in the near future.

(4) Delta Airlines depreciates its aeroplanes over ten years while United Airlines depreciates over a period as long as sixteen years. Again differences in depreciation write-off periods are very common.

The above has served to show that there is a wide amount of discretion left to accountants in calculating earnings and book net worth and these can lead to vastly differing results. This point is emphasised in the Forbes article cited above which contained the following quote by the chairman of the Sheraton Corporation, Mr Ernest Henderson: 'My earnings, sir, are what you say they are.' This variety of accounting treatments makes the basic interpretation of accounts and the comparing of accounts between different companies very difficult. Although inter-firm comparison is difficult, the generally accepted accounting principle of consistency should enable intra-company comparisons over various years to be made with a high level of reliability. If any firm makes any significant changes in its accounting policies, these should be specified in the accounts (required by S.S.A.P. 2 (1971)) and the impact shown. The creation of accounting standards under the auspices of the A.S.C. should lead to greater uniformity in accounting over time, although it is unlikely that these can ever be made precise enough to remove any uncertainty as to the treatment accorded to various transactions.

Some statistical studies have concluded that accounting data only provide a limited amount of new information and that investors can 'see through' the different accounting methods. One of the major studies was that by Ball,[7] who analysed the impact of

Table 3.1

Accounting magic (all 'In conformity with generally accepted accounting principles')

	Company A Col. 1	Company B's profits are higher because of						Company B Col. 8
		Use of FIFO in pricing inventory Col. 2	Use of straight-line depreciation Col. 3	Deferring research costs over 5 Years Col. 4	Funding only the pensions vested Col. 5	Use of stock options for incentive Col. 6	Including capital gain in income Col. 7	
Sales in units	100,000 units $100 each							100,000 units $100 each
Sales in dollars	$10,000,000							$10,000,000
Costs and expenses								
Cost of goods sold	$ 6,000,000							$ 6,000,000
Selling, general and administrative	1,500,000							1,500,000
LIFO inventory reserve	400,000	$(400,000)						
Depreciation	400,000		$(100,000)					300,000
Research costs	100,000			$(80,000)				20,000
Pension costs	200,000				$(150,000)			50,000
Officers' compensation								
Base salaries	200,000							200,000
Bonuses	200,000					$(200,000)		—
Total costs and expenses	$ 9,000,000	$(400,000)	$(100,000)	$(80,000)	$(150,000)	$(200,000)	—	$ 8,070,000
Profit before income taxes	$ 1,000,000	$ 400,000	$ 100,000	$ 80,000	$ 150,000	$ 200,000	—	$ 1,930,000
Income taxes	520,000	208,000	52,000	42,000	78,000	104,000	—	1,004,000
	$ 480,000 $0·80	$ 192,000 $0·32	$ 48,000 $0·08	$ 38,000 $0·06	$ 72,000 $0·12	$ 96,000 $0·16	—	$ 926,000
Gain on sale of property (net of income tax)	—						$150,000	150,000
Net profit reported	$ 480,000	$ 192,000	$ 48,000	$ 38,000	$ 72,000	$ 96,000	$150,000	$ 1,076,000
Per share on 600,000 shares	$0·80	$0·32	$0·08	$0·06	$0·12	$0·16	$0·25	$1·79

Market value at							
10 times earnings	$ 8·00	$3·20	$ ·80	$·63	$1·20	$1·60	$2·50	$17·93
12 times earnings	$ 9·60	$3·84	$ ·96	$·76	$1·44	$1·92	$3·00	$21·52
15 times earnings	$12·00	$4·80	$1·20	$·95	$1·80	$2·40	$3·75	$26·90

( ) denotes deduction.

Explanation of columns 2–7

Column	Company A	Company B
2	Uses LIFO (last-in, first-out) for pricing inventory.	Uses FIFO (first-in, first-out).
3	Uses accelerated depreciation for book and tax purposes.	Uses straight-line.
4	Charges research and development costs to expense currently.	Capitalises and amortises over five-year period.

(If research and development costs remain at same level, the difference disappears after five years. The difference of $80,000 in the chart is in the first year, where *A* expenses $100,000, and *B* capitalises the $100,000 but amortises 1/5.)

Column	Company A	Company B
5	Funds the current pension costs – i.e., current service plus amortisation of past service.	Funds only the present value of pensions vested.

(Difference in pension charges might also arise where, as in the case of U.S. Steel in 1958, management decides that current contributions can be reduced or omitted because of excess funding in prior years and/or increased earnings of the fund or the rise in market value of the investments.)

Column	Company A	Company B
6	Pays incentive bonuses to officers in cash.	Grants stock options instead of paying cash bonuses.
7	Credits gains (net of tax thereon) directly to earned surplus (or treats them as special credits below net income).	Includes such gains (net of income tax thereon) in income.

changes in accounting practice on share prices. The specific accounting practices he looked at included changes in depreciation policy, inventory valuation methods, consolidating subsidiaries, investments and the allocation of revenue into accounting periods. Using a sample of 197 firms making 267 changes in accounting practice between 1947 and 1961, Ball found that any 'adverse impact' of the change had already been anticipated in the stock price. Chapter 8 looks at studies into accounting information in greater detail.

Although there are obvious inconsistencies in accountancy practice, probably the major area of improvement that could be made is that of disclosure. Analysts require more and more information on past transactions and also on management's projections of future profitability. Although the latter is open to abuse, many analysts contend that company officials would rarely do this as they will be easily found out; additionally, analysts say that over time they will be able to recognise under- and over-optimistic forecasting companies. Another area in which accounting could be improved is for the firm to give as additional information the impact of alternative accounting treatments, for example to state what the net profits would have been if an alternative treatment had been used.

RATIOS

In interpreting basic accounting information, ratios are often constructed which help comparisons with prior-period data or data from rival firms or an industrial average. When using intercompany analysis, of course the analysts must be aware of the caveats about accounting practices mentioned previously. Amongst the most common ratios in use are:

(1) *Profitability ratios* – profit margins, return on capital employed, sales to capital employed, movements in asset value per share, and movements in earnings per share;

(2) *Efficiency ratios* – inventory or stock turnover, credit granted to debtors;

(3) *Liquidity ratios*; and

(4) *Gearing ratios*.

Breaking Down a Firm's Activities

The analysis of past annual reports and accounts and the examination of any press-cutting file will give a quick impression of the company's performance. These sources will give the analyst (new to analysing the particular firm) an idea of industries within which the company operates, the markets in which it sells, possible constraints on expansion, the financial structure of the company and critical factors which affect profitability. The analyst will probably summarise up to, say ten years of financial data and examine them for trends, compare them against competing firms in the same industry(ies) and compare them against industrial and economic indices. This examination and comparison should shed some light on the company's performance over time. In using annual accounting data the analyst should of course be aware of the concepts and conventions used in accounting and the scope these give for differing interpretations (this aspect was covered above).

The analyst will now have to concentrate on particular items to examine and to forecast. These items are obviously those that are of significance in a firm's revenue, cost and asset structure. The major starting-point in the forecasting process is that of sales turnover. This forms the main parameter to a firm's growth; costs are a function of sales (even fixed costs are eventually variable to sales) and assets are a function of sales (for example plant and machinery, inventories and debtors). Turnover should be broken down according to both the product type and the markets served. This is because the product type usually has a somewhat different cost structure and the market served is the parameter for sales (i.e. to calculate the demand for the firm's product). Some firms, of course, only produce one product and sell to only one industry – this obviously simplifies the analysis for the analyst. The analyst can determine the sales, as above, via a number of analyses. The most common of these include studying the annual accounts for the breakdown of activities, looking at sales catalogues, trade journals, advertising brochures and talking to the company's management. Once an analyst has been appraising a particular company over some period of time, they will have built up a good picture of the firm's sales breakdown (and indeed of other items relating to the firm) and so only a monitoring system is required.

UTILISING TRADE AND ECONOMIC STATISTICS

The analyst will now have to forecast the future sales of each of the components of the breakdown and possibly their growth rates (similar methodologies apply in forecasting costs and other factors).

Two major 'quantitative' methods are to use trade and economic statistics and to extrapolate statistical trends. Trade statistics can be utilised as leading indicators when they are published regularly, i.e. if a firm's year end is December, then quarterly trade figures of sales published just after the end of each quarter will give some idea of the firm's fortunes well ahead of the published results. This will involve the analyst estimating what the firm's market share is, or the variability of the firm's sales as a function of the variability of the trade's sales. Trade statistics can also be forecast into the future by using some statistical time-series or regression forecasting technique. By utilising the estimate of the firm's market share on the forecast trade sales, the analyst can then get an initial guide for the future sales of the firm. The market share can be estimated from past data. The reason for forecasting trade statistics instead of those for the firm itself is that greater accuracy can usually be gained when using quantitative forecasting techniques. Some trade associations themselves prepare forecasts of future demand and these are often published in journals. The forecasting techniques used by the associations are often quite sophisticated[8] and may make use of confidential data supplied by member firms. This source of information can be extremely valuable to the analyst. In using trade statistics, and especially when extrapolating for longer-term forecasts, care should be taken to make adjustments, albeit subjectively, for specific factors. For example, if the firm being examined appears to have some important technological developments ready to come on stream, this may make the analyst adjust upwards the historical market share enjoyed by the firm.

The analyst has the task of identifying relevant trade and economic statistics and of determining the reliability and use that can be attached to them for purposes of forecasting a particular security's earnings. Often there are a multitude of relevant statistics facing the analyst and he has to choose the best or the best combination, the criterion being those that give the most accurate forecasts over the appropriate time horizon. As the time horizon alters so may the rankings of relevant statistics. Correlation measures between various statistics and the company's actual outcomes may be taken in helping determine relevant statistics. As a general rule statistics which are prepared regularly (say monthly), and published quickly after the date to which they relate, give the best leading indicator forecasts.

In some cases there may be no relevant industrial statistics available and so recourse will have to be made to general economic indices. Although there are industry-wide indices which are often published some time after the event to which they relate, they do provide broad parameters to a firm's growth and can give indications of possible trends and developments. General economic statistics are usually of more help in forecasting various cost functions and financial variables. For example, statistics relating to unemployment, wage levels, industrial output, banking, inflation levels and interest rates can give very valuable data to the analyst. Some of these statistical sources also give forecasts for future periods and these again provide valuable information.

When using published economic statistics the analyst may adjust these for seasonal and cyclical elements. Thus any time series which contains significant seasonal and cyclical variations may be adjusted so that the underlying trends can be established. Analysts usually examine time series for turning points, that is where, say, the monthly percentage increase in a statistic over that of a year earlier starts to decline. This may indicate a change in the underlying trend and may herald the start of a recession in sales. Again the analyst has to use his judgement on top of the mechanically produced forecast.

Generally it will be useful to forecast quantity sales made by the firm although this may be a difficult task. By calculating quantity sales the analyst will be able to estimate the underlying growth in sales and additionally may allow more reliable comparisons with industry statistics to be made (as these are often in quantity format).

OTHER CONSIDERATIONS

There are also various other considerations which analysts commonly have to evaluate in forecasting sales. Amongst these are the following:

(*a*) *Long term contracts.* In civil-engineering and heavy-engineering firms substantial amounts of their business is represented by long-term contracts where the final figure for profits cannot be precisely determined for several years. Thus, quite apart from having to estimate the profits from various contracts, the analyst also has to determine when these will be reported in the accounts (the stock market tends to put a premium on companies who report profits earlier rather than later). In the case of long-term contracts the analyst will need to know as precisely as possible the accounting treatment given to long-term contracts – although the major accounting bodies have made recommendations relating to the accounting treatment of long-term contracts, there still remains a fair degree of latitude. The best approach open to the analyst in evaluating the accounting procedures in use is to speak to the company management to see if they are willing to discuss the method they use.

(*b*) *Geographical location of the firm's activities.* A breakdown of sales by geographical location is required as the prevailing economic conditions overseas may be different to those existing in the United Kingdom. By recognising the geographical location, analysts can turn to appropriate statistical sources when attempting to forecast. The geographical location of a firm's operations may also have some impact on investors' perceived 'riskiness' of a share, for example some overseas countries have nationalised assets at little or no compensation and some countries have made the remittance of funds to the United Kingdom impossible. By determining the location of the firm's activities the analyst can make some subjective judgement on other countries' political stability and their policies towards U.K.-owned firms. The geographical location of a firm's activities can be broken down by reference to the annual reports and accounts of both the parent and subsidiaries, from company visits and from professional and financial literature sources.

(*c*) *A knowledge of foreign exchange rates* will help determine the earnings of companies who have overseas sales, import substantial overseas goods, and maintain assets abroad.

(*d*) *Indirect taxation and credit controls.* The volume sales of many products are very sensitive to changes in indirect taxation (i.e. V.A.T.). Additionally, changes in credit controls such as the deposits and the repayment periods associated with hire-purchase transactions can significantly influence sales volume. If there are sufficient data, the analyst can measure the impact by regression analysis but in most cases analysts usually use subjective judgement.

The above paragraphs have briefly covered the forecasting of sales. Similar considerations apply in forecasting costs. The analyst then has to combine the forecasts to produce earnings per share figures.[9]

QUANTITATIVE METHODS IN FORECASTING COMPANY PROFITS
In combining together the various forecasted individual items the

analyst can make use of quantitative model-building approaches. The major method that has been made use of by analysts is probabilistic modelling and simulation.[10]

Probabilistic forecasting[11] allows the analyst to incorporate numerous values for the items he is forecasting, and probabilities are attached to these factors. This will lead to a forecast of several earnings per share figures each with a probability of occurrence – this giving a clearer picture of a company's earnings – risk profile. The probabilistic approach allows the analyst to include all the outcomes he thinks are possible for a particular item and so he is not forced to ignore data he has already collected and evaluated. The method is explicit in that the outcomes and the appropriate probabilities (although often subjectively arrived at) have to be spelt out for the calculations to be made. In using single-point data for forecasting, the analyst ignores a lot of data, and additionally there is the danger that the single-point estimates are not mean values but extreme ones – this can easily happen if the analyst has biased views regarding the security.

Probabilistic forecasting can be especially useful in the longer term where various assumptions about corporate growth, economic conditions and political decisions are made. If, as it probably will be, the model is programmed for a computer, then the sensitivity of the results to various changes in assumptions can be measured. For example, we can measure the change in earnings per share if sales increase by 5 per cent and if the average bank interest rate for overdrafts goes up by 1 per cent. The probabilistic approach is especially important if there is a good deal of uncertainty about and if the difference between the highest possible outcome and the lowest possible outcome is high. The probabilistic outcomes, such as those in Figure 3.1, highlights all the possible outcomes and their probabilities of occurrence.

The basic procedure is for the analyst to build a model which shows the interrelationships of all the various revenues and all the various costs. Thus the detailed breakdown discussed earlier in the chapter is required. An example is shown in Figure 3.2.[12] Here the analyst specifies three possible outcomes and their probabilities for each of the items. The three possible outcomes relate to the high, median and low forecasts. The analyst can include as many possible outcomes for each factor as he thinks necessary (i.e. not just three outcomes). Additionally, it is up to the analyst in deciding how far

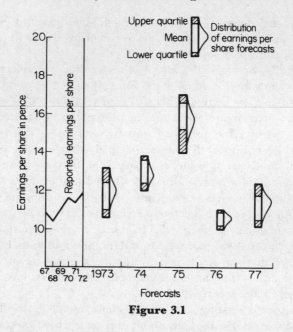

Figure 3.1

to break down the model – this could range from just ascertaining sales outcomes and attaching a percentage profit margin, to a detailed analysis where up to, say, ten individual items of costs may be included. The extent of the model depends very much upon the time and expense the analyst can afford and on the increase in forecasting accuracy obtained with the increased complexity. Although complex models require a lot of basic computation, this can easily be handled by computers. The major work-load is probably in building a satisfactory model and in fitting the relationships. In deriving a suitable model the analyst may well write out the relationships in the form of a probability tree. Once the model has been built the analyst can easily update his forecasts by using different probabilities and by varying the assumptions. The forecasts of possible outcomes are made using the analyses presented earlier in the chapter such as leading indicators. Instead of these being single point, however, a number of forecasts using the leading indicator can be made, i.e. using different market-share assumptions or different growth rates. The forecasting may also involve subjective adjustments being made to the mechanically produced forecast (i.e. those using statistical extrapolations).

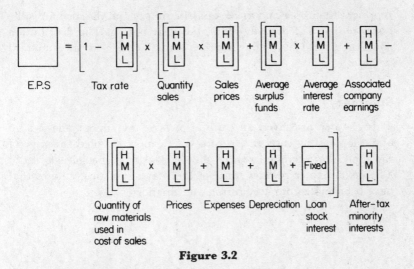

Figure 3.2

The analyst also has to specify probabilities of the possible outcomes. This may be done by looking at past history for probabilities of occurrence (for example of strikes) or by looking at past forecasting accuracy. By using past forecasting accuracy we can establish statistical confidence limits for future forecasts. In many cases the analyst may resort to subjective probabilities and this requires experience and sound judgement on his part. The feedback obtained from past forecasting accuracy will also help the analyst improve his estimates of appropriate probabilities – although this evolves over time and is of no relevance to a firm being evaluated for the first time.

Once the possible outcomes and the associated probabilities have been derived the calculation of the firm's earnings per share can be made. Thus the model expressed in Figure 3.2 is quantified and calculated. There will now be a number or range of earnings per share figures and whilst this will present the analyst with additional work in evaluating these, it will surely lead to a more accurate view of the earnings–risk profile of the company. Computers can be programmed to produce the earnings per share profile in pictorial form. Figure 3.1 shows an example.[13] The actual earnings per share are shown up to 1972 and then the distribution of forecast outcomes are shown up to the year 1977. The mean values are shown as a line through the hump of the distribution and the shaded areas represent the upper and lower quartile ranges and the median is the distance one half the way along the distribution. The distribution could of course have shown other statistics such as the standard deviation.

Summary

This chapter has given an outline of how investment analysts go about forecasting corporate profits. For a more detailed coverage of the topic the interested reader should consult a specialised text.[14] The next chapter reviews some of the major statistical studies that have been made into accounting and financial data.

CHAPTER 4

Statistical Models of Accounting Data

This chapter reviews major studies that have been made into the statistical structure of accounting data and especially those concerned with earnings per share. These studies have been carried out with the following aims in mind:

(1) to see if there is any underlying structure to earnings per share movements;

(2) to see if it is possible to predict earnings per share or other accounting data by statistical extrapolation; and

(3) to see if it is possible to predict bankruptcy, mergers and other occurrences from accounting data.

The Statistical Structure of Earnings Per Share Data – Theory

Four major earnings-generating models have been hypothesised and tested in the academic literature. First, there is the 'constant expectation' mean reverting process which implies that annual or periodic earnings remain constant over time, for example

$$\tilde{Y}_t = M + \tilde{U}_t, \tag{4.1}$$

where $\tilde{Y}_t$ = expected earnings in period t; this is a random variable at time $t - 1$. M = a constant value for earnings; that is the mean expected value of earnings over time is M. $\tilde{U}_t$ = random disturbance term or residual. This has a zero expected value, constant variance and is serially independent for all time periods. Thus it satisfies the usual assumptions of a linear regression model. The tilde denotes that the variable is random at time $t - 1$.

The equation says that the expected value of earnings in period t

will be equal to the value M. Thus, when measured over long periods of time, the earnings Y_t have a mean value of M. In individual years of course earnings will probably be above or below M and this is represented by the term $\hat{U}_t$. The mean reverting process implies that if, say, the $\hat{U}_t$ term is positive (i.e. earnings above those expected), then the $\hat{U}_t$ term of the following period will be negative (i.e. earnings below those expected) more often than not. The process therefore implies negative dependence or correlation between successive one-period earnings' changes.

In the majority of cases, however, firms will be reporting growth in earnings (if only through inflation). Thus the mean reverting process is adjusted so that the expectation of Y_t is not a constant but is a variable, for example a function of time. Thus the process defined in equation (4.1) becomes

$$\tilde{Y}_t = M_t + \hat{U}_t, \tag{4.2}$$

where M_t is some function, in this case, of time. This function could be based on a simple linear regression of earnings on time, i.e.

$$M_t = a + bT, \tag{4.3}$$

where T is the time period variable. Assuming that the equation was quantified as $M_t = 12 + 0.6T$, then the earnings per share would be 12p plus an increase of 0.6p in each time period. If the equation had been $M_t = 12 - 0.6T$, this means that earnings are declining throughout time; this is a possible, although far less common, occurrence.

Again the $\hat{U}_t$ term has a zero expectation and is mean reverting, and thus negative dependence is present in one-period earnings' changes. The mean of the first differences for the constant expectation model is zero; for the growth-decline model, the mean of the first differences will be non-zero (positive for growth models, negative for decline models).

The mean reverting processes are 'explained' on the grounds that many firms' earnings are either constant or follow a longer-term growth trend. Any large increases or decreases in earnings are regarded as being temporary and it is assumed that they will show a move in the opposite direction in the following year. In addition many accountants attempt to smooth profits under the above conditions and this has the impact of reducing the variability of earnings and keeping their values close to the mean.[1]

The third major model is that changes in earnings follow a martingale process. This process generates an independent series of earnings' changes and so the best estimate of the next period's earnings is the earnings of the period just passed; thus

$$\tilde{Y}_t = M_t + \tilde{U}_t \qquad (4.4)$$

and
$$M_t = Y_{t-1}. \qquad (4.5)$$

Therefore
$$E(\tilde{Y}_t) = Y_{t-1}, \qquad (4.6)$$

where E stands for 'expected value of'.

An earnings' series which follows a martingale process will behave as a series of random numbers – that is, there will be no systematic patterns or trends in the time series of earnings' changes. The successive one-period correlation between earnings' changes will be zero.

The fourth model which has been hypothesised to represent changes in earnings is the sub-martingale process. This superimposes the above martingale process on a general drift in earnings' changes, for example a general increase in changes in earnings may occur in times of booming economic conditions. In this case expression (4.6) becomes $E(\tilde{Y}_t) \geqslant Y_{t-1}$ for all time periods. Thus the expected value of earnings in period t will be equal to or larger than the earnings in period $t - 1$. The successive one-period correlation between earnings' changes are again zero. However, the mean of the first differences in the sub-martingale model will be non-zero whilst the mean in the martingale process will be zero.

In defence of the martingale model its protagonists claim persistence in earnings' growth rates is unlikely in a competitive economy. Thus few firms are able to enjoy long periods of above-average growth. Additionally, the earnings' figure is a residual of a host of business variables (revenues and costs) which contain various amounts of randomness. Therefore we may expect changes in earnings to be randomly distributed and therefore be represented by the martingale process. If there is a general change in earnings per share (i.e. through inflation) and the above martingale process is superimposed thereon, then the model follows a sub-martingale process.

The importance of recognising the type of process representing earnings' changes comes in attempting to predict earnings by statistical means. In the constant expectation or constant growth mean reverting models, past series of earnings' changes will be useful in predicting future values. For example, equation (4.3) allows us to predict future values of changes in earnings by substituting in the time-period value, T. The martingale model, however, says that the past history of earnings' changes are of no use in predicting future changes whilst the sub-martingale model says that past history of earnings' changes may be useful only in predicting the general drift in the values.[2]

The Statistical Structure of Earnings Per Share and other Accounting Data – Evidence

The first major study into the time-series behaviour of company earnings was that by Little[3] and followed up by Little and Rayner.[4] They correlated the annual growth rates of 529 quoted U.K. companies and found they were statistically independent. These findings proved a shock to most of the investment community, which thought that there were such things as long-term 'growth companies'. The evidence in fact suggested that either the martingale or sub-martingale models were appropriate for the time period covered.

Studies in the United States yield similar results. Lintner and Glauber[5] investigated the serial correlation of growth rates in sales, operating income, earnings before taxes and earnings per share of 309 companies listed on Compustat[6] tapes for the period 1946–65. They found very little statistical dependence in the variables looked at, and thus their findings agreed in large measure with those of Little and Rayner. Again these findings came as a shock to American investors. When analysing their results more closely, the authors found that the correlation between growth rates in successive periods was modestly positive for firms with the steadiest rates of growth – thus for a few companies, during some periods, there is significant dependence in changes in earnings. The authors replicated their own study on later data and derived similar conclusions.[7]

Murphy studied the correlation between relative rates of growth per share in successive periods for 344 companies spread across twelve industries between 1950 and 1965.[8] The periods he looked at were those of one-, two- and five-year periods and a five-year followed by a one-year period. Of his recordings 69 per cent showed no significant correlation, 25 per cent showed significant negative correlation and 6 per cent showed significant positive correlation. The negative correlation implied a mean reverting process, of course.

Brealey investigated the correlation between successive earnings changes of 700 American companies in the period 1951–64.[9] He found very little statistical dependence in earnings changes although what dependence there was, was often negative. Thus, as with Murphy's study above, a mean reverting process was implied for some companies. Brealey also conducted a runs test on the data and the actual number of runs were virtually the same as those expected under a random walk process. (Runs tests are those which measure the length and duration of plus signs or negative signs, i.e. the number of successive earnings' increases and the number of successive earnings' decreases. They are a fairly standard way of measuring statistical dependence and have been used in the share price studies reviewed in Chapter 7.)

Trent measured the correlation between successive growth rates of three ratios (earnings per share, return on ordinary share capital and return on total capital) and two absolute measures (sales and common equity) for 459 U.S. firms in the period 1946–52.[10] He found the correlation coefficients to be very small and non-significant.

Ball and Watts made a study of the twenty-year time-series behaviour of net earnings, earnings per share, net earnings divided by total assets and net sales of about 450 firms on the Compustat tapes.[11] Using serial correlation analysis, runs tests and 'partial-adjustment' models to examine the extent of the dependence of income expectation upon past income, they found that earnings and earnings per share series followed a sub-martingale process. Thus earnings and earnings per share exhibited independence in successive earnings' changes superimposed on an upward trend. Some commentators have noted that bias may be present in the results as Compustat corporations are generally large and successful and thus an increasing earnings trend may be expected (the problem of small sample bias is present in all studies using Compustat tapes).

Beaver also reported a study which correlated successive rates of return measures.[12] Three rates of return using stock market data in their construction were calculated and these were found to show significant negative correlation, thus providing support for the mean reverting process. Beaver also measured the serial correlation of one pure accounting determined variable, that of net earnings. This was found to follow a martingale process. A number of researchers have looked at various inflation-adjusted earnings' estimates to examine for dependence, the hypothesis being that these figures may be more predictable. The results have generally shown that inflation-adjusted earnings are no more predictable than historical cost figures.[13]

The studies have in general revealed that successive earnings changes are randomly distributed and can therefore be represented by a martingale or sub-martingale model. This means that there are no simple statistical rules which can be used to predict future earnings changes (note the sub-martingale model allows that historical values of earnings' changes may be used in determining the general drift or growth trend in earnings). However, the studies have also revealed that some firms have shown significant dependence in earnings changes,[14] and thus the investment analyst should look at each individual company to see if their past earnings record (or other accounting data, for example sales) can be used in predicting the future values (various mathematical expressions should be fitted to the data to see if they fit).

Some effort should be made to see if the inclusion of another variable(s) to the basic earnings prediction model will improve its forecasting accuracy. One example is a study by Peles,[15] who examined the effect of current advertising on future sales in various industries. The relationship so derived and current data relating to advertising expenditures allow a conditional expectation of future sales and earnings to be made.

A number of researchers have established that earnings are cross-sectionally positively correlated, i.e. that firms tend to, say, increase their earnings altogether in a particular year.[16] This is expected as companies are very dependent upon general economic conditions for their earnings (i.e. money supply, government spending, credit restrictions, affecting firms in like manner). This finding is also consistent with the existence of positive correlation between individual share prices and the market index (see Chapter 5). From this finding it is possible to predict individual company earnings movement given an earnings movement figure for the market generally. There have been no reported studies of the success of this prediction device – it is likely to be only a general indicator, however, and no precise reliance should be placed on it.

Predicting Annual Earnings from Mechanical Extrapolations of Interim Reports

A number of studies have been made into the accuracy of predicting corporate annual earnings from mechanical extrapolations of interim reports. Most of these studies have extrapolated quarterly earnings reports by a number of standard statistical functions and tested whether they lead to better forecasts of annual earnings (as opposed to not using the quarterly data).

Green and Segall made a study of the predictive quality of forty-six first-quarter reports of earnings per share (E.P.S.) in 1964.[17] A number of statistical extrapolations were employed to compare annual E.P.S. forecasts that incorporated first-quarter reports with forecasts that did not use interim report information. (For example, one extrapolation was that earnings for 1964 would differ from those of 1963 by the same percentage that the first-quarter earnings for 1964 differed from the first-quarter earnings for 1963.) The results were somewhat surprising as the forecasts which used the first-quarter earnings' announcements were not superior to those that did not use the information. This is against what we would expect as by using first-quarter announcements we are only forecasting nine months ahead, whilst without using the announcement we are forecasting for twelve months. Recognising the surprising nature of the results, Green and Segall repeated their study and extended the data used.[18] They reached similar conclusions, however, and said 'We see no reason to modify the weasel-like conclusion of the original paper, "First-quarter reports as presently prepared are of little help in forecasting earnings per share". '

Subsequent researchers, however, have found at least some small amount of predictive ability in mechanically extrapolating first-quarter earnings' figures. Brown and Niederhoffer, for example, replicated Green and Segall's analyses on a sample of 519 corporations for the years 1962–5 listed on Compustat tapes.[19] In contrast to the earlier studies of Green and Segall, Brown and Niederhoffer found that interim reports are useful in forecasting future annual earnings and gave better predictions than if the interim report had been ignored. Further, they found that the predictability increased with each new interim report. Whilst it is difficult to account for the differences,[20] Brown and Niederhoffer's study used a far larger sample and over a wider period than did Green and Segall. Additionally, of course, Brown and Niederhoffer's results are intuitively correct and subsequent studies by other researchers have confirmed their findings. Amongst these further studies are those by Coates;[21] Brown and Kennelly,[22] who used a residuals analysis approach (see Chapter 7 for this type of research methodology); Reilly, Morgenson and West,[23] who measured the predictive ability of first-quarter reports for annual earnings, net profit margins and sales; Latané, Tuttle and Jones;[24] and Jones and Litzenberger.[25] Most of these studies, as indeed do many of the studies reported in this chapter, use Compustat tapes and so the sample data are largely the same; additionally, they cover the larger and more successful firms. (This is no very bad thing, however, as it is these firms which have the most economic impact on society – research is still required of course on small firms.)

There now seems to be a fair consensus that mechanical extrapolation of interim reports leads to better predictions of annual earnings per share, and this is intuitively correct. However, even before the earliest of the above academic studies, virtually all practising analysts had been evaluating quarterly information on earnings, sales, and so on, and using it to help predict annual data. In addition, of course, analysts should be able to make better predictions using quarterly data than the academic studies above as they can include other data in their analyses. However, the academic studies have shown that even mechanical extrapolation has improved the predictability of annual earnings and has provided quantitative evidence that interim reports provide valuable information to the investment community. Although there have been no comparable studies in the United Kingdom, it seems certain that, apart from the costs involved, quarterly reports would provide useful information to the stock market.[26] (At the moment very few U.K. firms issue quarterly reports. All quoted companies have to prepare and issue half-yearly statements, however.)

The Prediction of Corporate Failures, Creditworthiness and the Occurrences of Takeovers from Accounting Data

Another broad body of research studies has attempted to predict certain business occurrences such as bankruptcies, creditworthiness and mergers from accounting data. Accurate prediction of these occurrences is of obvious value both to the individuals involved (company management, lenders, banks, investors) as well as to society at large (for example to mitigate or prevent the 'social' losses occurring from bankruptcies). The basic methodology is to determine the 'accounting data' characteristics of, say, bankrupt or taken-over companies prior to that occurrence, which differentiated them (with a certain level of statistical significance)[27] from non-bankrupt or non-taken-over firms, i.e. if the differentiating characteristic of a taken-over firm one year prior to the bid was a return on capital employed of 7 per cent or under, then any firm in the future which earns a return of 7 per cent or under will be regarded as a strong possibility for takeover. Most of the models have used accounting data solely – this is because it is objective and quantifiable. In practice a credit or investment analyst will use various qualitative factors and personal judgement on top of the quantitative prediction given by the model. If it is possible to quantify the non-accounting data, then these should be included in the models, or at least tested to see if they improve the model's explanatory or predictive abilities. Some of the research studies have used univariate analyses, i.e. where there is just one financial characteristic being used to differentiate the group of companies (for example takeover and non-takeover). Others have used multi-variate analyses where there are a number of financial characteristics which, combined together, differentiate between groups. The major multivariate technique used to date has been multiple discriminant analysis (M.D.A.). An example of the use of M.D.A. is given later when reference is made to Altman's Study.[28]

There have been many attempts at building prediction models over the past forty years, although they mainly relate to U.S. data. The next few sections briefly review some of the major reported studies.

COMPANY FAILURES

The successful prediction of company failures is of obvious benefit to credit analysts and investment analysts and hence they have devoted considerable time to this quest. Amongst the earliest of the quantitative studies into corporate bankruptcy was that by Ramser and Foster,[29] who analysed eleven different financial ratios of 173 firms in Illinois. They found that the less successful firms and those that subsequently failed had poorer financial ratios than the successful firms. Further studies by Fitzpatrick,[30] Winakor and Smith,[31] Merwin,[32] and Saulnier, Halcrow and Jacoby[33] corroborated the findings from Ramser and Foster's study although they included various other financial ratios in their various researches. Moore and Atkinson[34] and Seiden[35] also used accounting data and ratios in determining the ability of firms to obtain trade credit. They found significant evidence linking poor financial characteristics with difficulty in obtaining credit, thus indicating that credit analysts recognised the warning signs (they had possibly read the above-mentioned studies). The ratios used in the studies varied but they were usually some version of fairly standard measures such as cash flow/total debt, current ratio, quick assets ratio, working capital/ total assets, total debt/total assets and the movements in the above measures over time. The researchers used a univariate approach and did not therefore measure the combined impact of all the ratios. Unfortunately few of the studies actually built a prediction model which was tested on future data.

One of the first researchers to directly build and test a prediction model for company bankruptcy was Beaver.[36] His data consisted of seventy-nine firms that had either become bankrupt or had defaulted on interest and dividend payments (one had an over-drawn bank account). In addition, seventy-nine non-failed paired firms[37] were selected for comparison purposes. Thirty conventional financial ratios using data over a five-year period were extracted for each of the seventy-nine failed firms and for each of the seventy-nine non-failed paired firms. The mean ratios of each failed firm were compared against those of each non-failed paired firm. Beaver found substantial evidence of failed firms suffering deteriorating financial ratios over the five-year period and they were substantially worse than the paired non-failed firm: 'the deterioration in the means of the failed firms is very pronounced over the five year period. . . . The evidence overwhelmingly suggests that there is a difference in the ratios of failed and non-failed firms.'

Beaver then tested which ratios were the best predictors of company failure across all companies. A number of predictability techniques were used including the dichotomous classification test. For example, it seems plausible that for each pair the firm with the poorest current ratio is likely to fail; thus from each pair the firm with the lowest current ratio is predicted to fail. This categorisation is then compared with the actual outcome and the percentage of errors in classification measured. (A model with no predictive accuracy at all would, on average, mis-classify 50 per cent of the time. The predictive model must certainly gain greater accuracy than this if it is to be in any way valid.) Using such an approach Beaver found that the 'cashflow to total debt ratio' gave the most successful predictions (i.e. the least number of wrong answers). The percentage of errors came to 22 per cent when the ratio was measured five years before failure and 10 per cent when measured in the year before. The current ratio, a very popular measure of solvency in financial literature, was in fact a poorish predictor with a much higher percentage of mis-classifications (20 per cent of firms mis-classified using data one year prior to the failure and 31 per cent mis-classified using data five years prior).

In a later study Beaver compared the predictive ability of financial ratios with those of stock market prices.[38] The hypothesis here was that stock market prices may provide better predictions as the prices impound all the available knowledge relating to a security and not just accounting data. Beaver found that stock market prices gave more warning of corporate bankruptcy than did accounting data. The difference was quite small, however, with the average length of time from the date of failure forecast to the failure date being 2·45 years when using share prices and 2·31 years when using accounting data (net income/total assets being the ratio used). The investigation was somewhat limited in scope, and even Beaver himself warned about reading too much into the results.

Another univariate approach to predicting business failure is the use of a behavioural model of the firm. Using such a model based on a markov chain process, Wilcox showed that it gave good predictions on a sample of paired failed and non-failed firms.[39]

The major initial studies on the use of multivariate models in predicting corporate failure are those by Altman.[40] Altman used multiple discriminant analysis (M.D.A.),[41] which is a technique that classifies an observation (for example a firm) into one of several *a priori* groupings (for example failed and non-failed) depending upon the observation's specific characteristics (for example financial ratios such as current ratio and growth in earnings). The multiple discriminant analysis then gives a linear combination of some or all of these characteristics that best differentiates or discriminates between the groups. The discriminant function can be expressed thus:

$$Z = b_1 X_1 + b_2 X_2 + b_3 X_3 + \ldots b_n X_n,$$

where b_1, b_2, b_3, $\ldots b_n$ = discriminant coefficients and X_1, X_2, X_3, $\ldots X_n$ = independent variables (in Altman's study these were various financial ratios), and Z = the discriminant score.

The discriminant score, Z, for any particular firm is then compared against predetermined cut-off points which classify the firm into two or more groups (in Altman's study, failed or non-failed). The cut-off points are set in relation to past prediction accuracy.

The data used in Altman's study consisted of thirty-three pairs of manufacturing firms (a non-failed firm being compared against a paired failed firm) where size and industry were used as the criteria for pairing. Altman selected the same twenty-two accounting and non-accounting data variables for each company which he thought may help in explaining and predicting corporate failure. The discriminant model then derived the combination of variables that best discriminated between failed and non-failed firms. This produced a discriminant function with just five independent variables (the other seventeen being of no value in the model); thus

$$Z = 0{\cdot}012X_1 + 0{\cdot}014X_2 + 0{\cdot}033X_3 + 0{\cdot}006X_4 + 0{\cdot}999X_5,$$

where X_1 = working capital/total assets, X_2 = retained earnings/total assets, X_3 = earnings before interest and taxes/total assets, X_4 = market value of equity/book value of total debt, X_5 = sales/total assets, and Z = overall index (discriminant score).

The cut-off points for Z established by Altman were thus: all firms that had a Z score greater than 2·99 fell into the non-bankrupt class and all firms with a Z score smaller than 1·81 fell into the bankrupt category. Z scores which fell between 1·81 and 2·99 contained both bankrupt and non-bankrupt firms; in using the model for prediction purposes an analyst would have to use his judgement in categorising a firm into fail and non-fail groups if they have a Z score between 1·81 and 2·99.

An example of the use of Altman's model is given below:

In evaluating A Ltd via Altman's model the following ratios were extracted:

$$X_1 = 40 \text{ per cent}$$
$$X_2 = 10 \text{ per cent}$$
$$X_3 = 20 \text{ per cent}$$
$$X_4 = 200 \text{ per cent}$$
$$X_5 = 0.6$$

Thus the Z score is computed

$$Z = 0.012(40) + 0.014(10) + 0.033(20) + 0.006(200) + 0.999(0.6)$$
$$Z = 3.08.$$

The Z score of 3·08 indicates that the firm is in reasonable financial health and there is no indication of any bankruptcy problems.

In practical applications of corporate failure prediction models the bank or other interested party should build their own models based on the data they have available, Altman's data being fairly small on which to base universal acceptance of his model. Additionally, the form of the model, its discriminant coefficients and the cut-off points in the Z score should be re-evaluated over time as conditions change. Of course analysts can always add their subjective judgement of a situation on top of the quantitative 'answer' given by the model.

Altman tested the predictive accuracy of his model by employing similar techniques to Beaver (see p. 74). Using data from one year before the bankruptcy for constructing the five variables, Altman found that 95 per cent of the sample were correctly classified as failed or non-failed. When data from two years prior to the bankruptcy were used, the correct classification fell to 72 per cent (however, this does give two year's warning). When data prior to two years before the failure were used, the prediction accuracy fell away sharply such that it was not very different from a random choice (i.e. 50 per cent correct classification). Altman also tested the model on a different sample and found the predictive accuracy to be good – 96 per cent correct classification being reported when using data one year before bankruptcy. Taffler has recently reported a similar success in predicting bankruptcies when using an M.D.A. model in the United Kingdom.[42] The model was developed for a private stockbroking firm and hence his article did not publish the discriminant coefficients.

Another well-referenced study into the prediction of corporate failure was that by Meyer and Pifer.[43] They used a linear probability model instead of M.D.A. This involves building a regression equation which contains both independent variables made up of financial ratios (i.e. working capital) and a dependent 'dummy' variable. This 'dummy' variable was assigned a value of 0 for solvent firms and 1 for those which became bankrupt. The model then yields the best model which discriminates between failed and non-failed firms – thus the method arrives at results which are similar to those produced by discriminant analysis.[44]

Meyer and Pifer used this methodology in predicting bank failures, their data consisting of thirty-one pairs of banks in the period 1948–65. The pairing criteria were that the banks be situated in the same city, be of approximately the same size and age and be subject to the same regulatory controls. Thirty-two variables were tested as being of possible predictive value. When using data one or two years prior to the failure, approximately 80 per cent of the observations were correctly classified. When data prior to this were used the financial variables were unable to successfully discriminate between viable and failing banks.

Westerfield made a study of the share price movements of twenty bankrupt firms for ten years prior to the failure.[45] Using a residual analysis approach (see p. 128) he found that the share prices had shown abnormally (i.e. unexpectedly) bad performance for as far back as five years before the bankruptcy. This implies that the firms involved started to report poor earnings' performance and poorish earnings' prospects for a number of years prior to the bankruptcy and that investors recognised this. However, Westerfield's study did not involve building a prediction model.

The evidence to date has shown that accounting data and financial ratios measured from a period as long as two years before failure differ between failed and non-failed firms. Additionally, the models have been shown to have good predictive ability. However, the following points must be borne in mind:

(1) The various studies,[46] whilst often considering similar-type ratios, have all ended up with different models[47] and with different weightings and with different cut-off points.

(2) The control groups (the pairs) used in the research have always been the same in number as the group being investigated.

There is no statistical or practical reason that requires the control group to be the same size, and indeed by increasing the numbers in the control group the sampling errors of the estimates of the non-failed firms' financial ratios and characteristics will decrease.

(3) Most of the models have paired firms in relation to size and industry and thus these characteristics have been omitted from consideration as predictor variables. However, there may be some relationship here (indeed recent experience in the United Kingdom has suggested that some industries are more vulnerable than others to company bankruptcy, for example building firms).

(4) A majority of the models have not included non-accounting data. For example, the age of a firm has not been included in many models even though there is evidence from elsewhere that this is associated with business failure.[48]

(5) There have been few reported research results on the predictive value of the models when applied to future data. The evidence from (1) above would seem to indicate that the characteristics of failed firms change across time and thus that models have to be re-evaluated. If the parameters and the form of the model change very rapidly, then the predictive value may be minimal.

CREDITWORTHINESS – EVALUATION OF LONGER-TERM LOANS

Prediction models using financial data have also been derived in bond evaluation (bonds being fixed-interest securities – i.e. equivalent to debentures and loan stocks in the United Kingdom; recently there have been moves in the United Kingdom to formally grade debentures and loan stocks – it is still at a planning stage in 1976). Examples of these include models which have determined the risk premium of bonds (i.e. the excess return over the risk-free rate earned) and those that have predicted the formal gradings given to bonds by credit agencies. An example of the former is the work of Fisher.[49] He postulated a four-factor model, the basic form of which, along with its parameters, was as follows:

$$X = 0.987 + 0.307Y_1 - 0.253Y_2 - 0.537Y_3 - 0.275Y_4,$$

where X = the risk premium; Y_1 = the riskiness of a firm's earnings – this was taken as the coefficient of variation of the firm's net income over a period of nine years; Y_2 = a measure of the reliability of the firm in meeting its obligations – this was taken as the length of time since the latest event of: the firm being founded, the firm emerging from a bankruptcy, the firm making a compromise with its creditors; Y_3 = a measure of the capital-structure riskiness – this was taken as the equity/debt ratio; the equity figure was taken as the stock market value of the equity shares; Y_4 = a measure of the marketability of the bonds – this was taken as the total market value of the bonds.

The coefficient of multiple determination, R^2, was 0·75, a reasonably good fit, and all the independent variables were significant. However, Fisher did not test the predictive ability of the model – thus there has been no evidence published on whether managements who are considering issuing bonds can accurately forecast the terms on which to make an issue (it seems reasonable that at least some small predictive accuracy should be obtained). Obviously, if management could accurately forecast risk premiums, it would enable their selection of capital structure to be that much more efficient. Equally investors in bonds would benefit from using a reliable bond premium model (until the benefits get discounted away of course).

In the United States marketable bonds are graded by various credit agencies which employ many expert analysts to make the evaluations. The rating corresponds to the analysts' opinions of the probability of default in interest and principal payments (some weighting may also be applied to other factors, for example marketability). A number of research studies have been carried out on the success of the ratings.[50] The results have shown that the ratings given by the agencies are good guides to the future behaviour of bonds.

In evaluating bonds analysts rely upon making detailed analyses of the firm involved and use both past data and future prospects. Apparently few agencies rely upon any formal prediction model-building in their evaluations, and in backing this up some have gone on record as saying that such quantitative methods would give very poor results.[51] However, a number of academics have thought otherwise and have attempted to build models which give identical ratings to those produced by the agencies. The advantages of deriving a successful model include quicker evaluations, consistency in evaluations and cost savings through replacing many of the 'expert' analysts. Horrigan was amongst the first to develop a model for bond gradings.[52] His model, based on bond ratings given by

Moody's and Standard & Poor's (two bond grading agencies) to 215 different firms in the period 1959–64, was of the following form:

$$Y = b_1 X_1 + b_2 X_2 - b_3 X_3 + b_4 X_4 - b_5 X_5,$$

where Y = bond ratings (Standard & Poor's have twelve ratings in their system), X_1 = total assets, X_2 = shareholders' equity to total debt, X_3 = working capital to sales – this turned out to have an inverse relationship with the bond rating, X_4 = operating profit to sales, X_5 = sales to net worth – this had a negative association with the bond rating.

The coefficient of multiple determination, R^2, was slightly below 0·5 for the various samples examined.

Horrigan used the coefficients derived from his sample to predict new sets of ratings (i.e. for those firms issuing new bonds) and to predict changes in existing ratings. The independent variables, X_1 to X_5, were the financial data relating to the firm one and two years prior to the new rating or the change in rating. The results showed that approximately 58 per cent of Moody's and 52 per cent of Standard & Poor's new ratings were correctly classified and that most of the remaining predictions were within one rating of the actual. Approximately 54 per cent of Moody's and 57 per cent of Standard & Poor's rating changes were correctly predicted by the model. These results showed a reasonable amount of predictive ability, although, as Horrigan emphasised, its main success lay in determining new bond ratings as opposed to timing and predicting changes in bond ratings. Horrigan adapted his model to include a subordination factor[53] – this being a dummy variable as it is a qualitative measure. This improved the R^2 considerably with the figure rising to over 0·6 and the t statistic of the subordination variable was highly significant.

In another study on bonds West used Fisher's model and data (see p. 79) to predict the ratings given by the credit-ranking agencies.[54] He found that the model accounted for more than 70 per cent of the variability in the logarithms of the ratings and predicted correctly about 60 per cent of the ratings given by the agencies. Pinches and Mingo also carried out a study on industrial bond ratings and their model correctly predicted the ratings in 64 per cent of cases.[55] They used a discriminant analysis approach with seven variables. (They originally postulated thirty-five variables but this was reduced to just seven important factors. This was done by using factor analysis, which is a technique that breaks down the independent variables into the important items.) Other research on bond ratings include those by Pogue and Soldofsky,[56] Carleton and Lerner[57] and Horton.[58]

The evidence of the above research suggests that bond ratings can be predicted fairly well from financial models. The difference in the rankings as given by the bond ratings and by the prediction models may in fact be wholly or more likely partially the result of poor grading by the agencies – they have not been found to be infallible. In this regard future research may be more directed to building prediction models of bond defaults as opposed to predicting bond ratings (which are not entirely accurate). The major predictor variables incorporated in the models were those relating to risk, although the marketability of the bond was also of some importance.

CREDITWORTHINESS – BANK LENDING

A number of researchers have attempted to build models to explain and help determine credit evaluation by banks. Most of the models have related to private individuals and only a few have been directed towards business entities – the lack of research in the latter is due largely to the inadequacy of available information."[9] Amongst the earliest of the corporate customer credit evaluation studies was that by Hester.[60] He built two types of model, one relating to the characteristics of the loan applicant and one to the characteristics of the lending bank. Thus:

$$F_1(R, M, A, S) = f(W_1, W_2, \ldots W_I) \qquad (4.1)$$
$$F_2(R, M, A, S) = f(Z_1, Z_2, \ldots Z_J) \qquad (4.2)$$

where R = the loan rate of interest (in per cent), M = the maturity of the loan (in months), A = the amount of the loan (in dollars), $S = 1$ if the loan is secured, 0 otherwise, W_i = the ith relevant characteristic of loan applicants $(i = 1, 2, \ldots I)$, Z_j = the jth relevant characteristic of lending banks $(j = 1, 2, \ldots J)$.

Data for model (4.1) were extracted from the corporate customers of three large banks which raised loans of over one year's duration in the period January 1955 through to October 1957. The data consisted of items relating to the borrower's financial position and the past creditworthiness of the firm with the bank. The results of the regressions revealed that four financial items were significant in explaining bank lending terms, these being average profits calculated over a three- or five-year period (depending upon the availability of data), current ratio, average bank balance, and the ratio of profits to total assets. For model (4.1) the R^2 statistics for each dependent variable averaged over the three banks were as follows:

interest rate	0·77
loan duration	0·35
amount of loan	0·49
requirement of security	0·24

Thus the model's best fit came when the rate of interest was being 'explained'.

Data for model (4.2) came from a large number of banks making loans to businesses in the period 1955 to 1957. These consisted of the level of deposits, the ratio of commercial and industrial loans to total assets, and a dummy location variable (all relating to the bank), and the borrower's total assets. The R^2 were lower than those of model (4.1) and thus a bank's characteristics appear to be a smaller influence in the setting of lending terms than the characteristics of the borrowing firms. The borrowers' total assets turned out to be the most significant variable in model (4.2).

Other major research studies in building prediction models for credit and loan evaluation include those by Cohen, Gilmore and Singer,[61] Wojnilower,[62] Wu[63] and Orgler.[64] Cohen *et al.*'s study attempted to simulate, and hence predict, bank managers' lending decisions as opposed to predicting defaulting loans. The research looked at the entire loan-evaluation procedure and not just at the use of financial statements in the credit-granting process. The authors found that simulation was of use both in helping train new loans managers and because it could probably be developed to improve the loan-analysis process.

Wojnilower found that bank lending officers' decisions could be predicted fairly well from a study of the borrower's financial positions and their past creditworthiness record. Wu's study found that bank lending officers had a good record in classifying loans. From this he concluded that the building of models predicting bank lending officers' decisions would be very useful because of cost savings and because of the consistency that could be gained. Orgler's study also attempted to predict bank lending officers' decisions. He used various financial features (i.e. whether the loan was secured or not) as his independent variables. Although the R^2 was rather poor at 0·364, the model managed to perform reasonably well when predicting whether loan applications would be graded as uncriticised (i.e. good lending situations), marginal and criticised (i.e. risky lending situations).

PREDICTION OF TAKEOVERS

Researchers have also used accounting data in attempting to explain and predict likely takeover targets. As takeovers and mergers take place at a time when share prices of the participating companies are moving around by large amounts, successful prediction can lead to significant stock market profits, and many investors have joined in this quest. Most of the reported studies have been conducted by academics, however.

Singh conducted a study into U.K.-quoted companies taken over in the period 1955–60.[65] Using both univariate and discriminant analysis, Singh found that the taken-over firms tended to have low profitability, low growth and low valuation ratios (defined as market capitalisation divided by shareholders' equity) when compared against non-taken-over companies. Singh found that bidding companies had a significantly higher level of growth than the firms taken over. Kuehn's study, which consisted of takeovers of quoted firms in the United Kingdom in the period 1957–69,[66] used a linear probability model and probit analysis to explain the characteristics of firms engaged in takeovers. Kuehn found that taken-over firms had low valuation ratios (by far the most important variable), low profitability, low growth and poor liquidity. He also found that the bidding firms had higher growth in net assets and higher valuation ratios than the industry average. Tzoannos and Samuels used financial characteristics in a discriminant analysis approach to explaining thirty-six randomly chosen takeovers in the period July 1967 to March 1968.[67] The R^2 for the financial characteristics of the taken-over firms was rather low at 0·24 but the R^2 for the financial characteristics of the bidders was more substantial at 0·53. Tzoannos and Samuels concluded:

> It was found that the characteristics possessed by those companies that were taken over, which differentiated them from the companies not taken over, were as follows: a higher absolute level of

capital gearing, a higher rate of increase in the capital gearing, a slower increase in profits, a lower price earnings ratio, a slower rate of increase in dividends and a greater variation over time in the rate of dividends.

The characteristics of the companies that were active in taking over other companies were an above average downward trend in capital gearing, a lower absolute level of capital gearing, a higher than average increase in profits to capital employed and a higher than average increase in the trend of dividends.

The above research followed an earlier study by the authors.[68] In this they found that taken-over firms tended to be undervalued by the stock market when using the Weaver–Hall model (which was described in Chapter 2, p. 35). They attempted to use the Weaver–Hall model in their later study but they found that the regression model was so unsound on the new data that this approach was abandoned.

Other, univariate, studies were made by Newbould[69] and Buckley[70] Both found that taken-over firms had poor earnings' growth and low price–earnings ratios prior to the takeover. Unlike Buckley, Kuehn and Singh, however, Newbould did not find that the taken-over firms had suffered low valuation ratios.

The latest study on the financial characteristics of takeovers in the United Kingdom was that by the present author.[71] The population consisted of 120 bids for quoted companies made in 1973. A multiple discriminant analysis model, consisting of four variables, the valuation ratio, profitability, growth and activity, was found to give a statistically significant explanation of takeovers. These variables indicated that it is generally the poorer performing firms which are taken over. The model was found to give good predictions of takeovers when applied to a future set of observations.

Similar studies to those in the United Kingdom have been carried out in the United States. Taussig and Hayes made a study of cash takeovers in the United States with the aim of identifying any common financial features.[72] Their data consisted of a random selection of fifty cash takeovers in the period 1956–70. The financial characteristics of this sample were then compared against a randomly chosen control group consisting of fifty non-acquired firms. The authors found that acquired firms had high liquidity, poor earnings and a declining dividend policy.

Another study on U.S. data was made by Stevens, who measured the financial characteristics of forty companies which were taken over in the year 1966.[73] Using factor analysis and discriminant analysis, he examined the data and found it was possible to predict the financial structures of acquired companies; subsequent validation testing proved the results. The major discriminating features were a lower level of gearing and highish liquidity. Stevens concluded:

> These findings imply that financial characteristics alone provide a means by which acquired firms can be separated from others. Therefore, one can argue that, regardless of the stated motive for merger, financial characteristics either are explicit decision variables or directly reflect non-financial reasons for acquisition. In addition, the firm's capital structure appears to be an especially important variable, both by itself and in a profile with variables measuring liquidity, profitability and activity.

The third research study was that conducted by Monroe and Simkowitz on conglomerate mergers in 1968.[74] Using a discriminant analysis approach, they found that acquired firms were smaller in size, had lower price–earnings ratios, lower dividend pay-out ratios and had a low growth in net assets.

The studies have shown that taken-over firms had low profitability and that they had low price–earnings ratios when measured prior to the takeover. Unfortunately none of the studies have derived formal prediction models. The research suggests, however, that the financial characteristics of the firms involved do change across time and hence any prediction model would have to be re-evaluated at frequent intervals.

Summary

This chapter has summarised some of the major quantitative studies on the statistical nature of published accounting data and on the performance of prediction models using these data. Most of the research has been conducted in the United States and so the reader should beware of automatically imputing these results to the U.K. situation.

Although the latest studies have shown that changes in earnings figures and some other accounting data are randomly distributed, research into the use of prediction models has found them to be of some predictive value. However, practising analysts tend to rely more heavily on their own individual judgement than the use of formal prediction models (many analysts use the model's results as one input into their judgement). Studies have suggested that analysts' evaluations tend to be better than those produced solely from mechanical prediction models (as perhaps they should be).

One point worth noting is that if the prediction models and their parameters became widely accepted, this may affect the event that is being predicted. For example, if a firm is classified as a takeover candidate, its price may rise such that it then becomes so expensive that it drops out of this grouping. Likewise, if a firm is predicted as a likely failure, this will deter investors and banks investing or lending to them. This in turn may hasten the bankruptcy (which may not have otherwise occurred) or it may make the firm adopt a safety-first approach which in turn may make it survive. It is doubtful if individual prediction models are widely believed in on an emphatic basis at the moment; if they were widely believed in, then research into the above problems would surely be required and the models would need to be re-evaluated at frequent intervals to ensure they remain valid and useful.

Thus accounting data, even when used in a mechanical sense, are of considerable use to their users. However, more research is needed in this area both in improving the predictive accuracy of the models and in examining their impact on economic events.

CHAPTER 5

The Capital Asset Pricing Model

With the growth in empirical studies into share price behaviour there has also been a concomitant search for an underlying theory which specifies the expected returns from individual securities. The outcome of this search has been the widespread acceptance of the capital asset pricing model (C.A.P.M.). The C.A.P.M. was developed by Sharpe,[1] Lintner[2] and Mossin,[3] and is based on the assumption that investors desire to hold securities' portfolios which are 'efficient' in that they provide maximum returns for given levels of risk (they act in the manner prescribed by portfolio theory).[4]

The C.A.P.M. as described by Sharpe rests upon a number of assumptions. These are the following:

(1) investors are risk averse;

(2) investors have identical time horizons and identical return expectations for each individual security;

(3) each investor can borrow or lend at the riskless rate of interest (which is the same for all investors);

(4) there are no taxes or transaction costs; and

(5) investors are rational in that they desire to hold efficient portfolios.

The assumptions are unrealistic in the real world and this may appear to invalidate the model. However, before we review the assumptions and the limitations they impose, a brief discussion of the model will be given.

Figure 5.1 shows the investment opportunities available to investors plotted on a risk–return basis. Rational risk-averse investors would choose portfolios on the upper left-hand boundary of the shaded area, this being known as the 'efficient frontier'. Because of the homogeneous expectations assumption there is just one

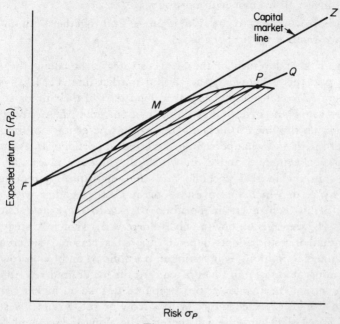

Figure 5.1

efficient frontier. All portfolios along this boundary provide maximum expected returns for their given level of risk.

When we include the assumption that all investors can borrow or lend at some riskless rate, F, which is determined outside the stock market, we increase the available investment opportunities. An investor can now lend or borrow at rate F and combine this with the investment in portfolio M to obtain any combination along the line FMZ (this is obtained by drawing a straight line through the point F tangential to the efficient frontier; point Z has no theoretical limit).

The point M is known as the market portfolio and it is the optimal combination of all risky securities. In equilibrium all securities will be included in portfolio M in proportion to their market values. Given the line FMZ an investor can

(1) lend all his money at the riskless rate F;

(2) lend part of his money at the riskless rate F and invest the remainder in the market portfolio M

(3) invest all his money in portfolio M;

(4) borrow money at the riskless rate F and together with any of his own funds invest in portfolio M.

The risk and return of the above strategies lie along the line FMZ and this is known as the capital market line (C.M.L.). The segment FM relates to investors who lend part of their funds at the riskless rate F and invest the remainder in portfolio M. An investor's position on the line FM depends upon what percentage of funds is lent at rate F and what percentage invested in portfolio M. Point M represents strategy 3 above, in which the investor invests all his money in the market portfolio and the segment MZ represents strategy 4, in which the investor borrows and together with any funds of his own invests in portfolio M (again the exact position along MZ depends on how much is borrowed). Which strategy an individual investor adopts depends upon his personal preferences and financial position; by investing in portfolio M and by borrowing or lending at rate F, an investor can attain his desired risk–return combination. An investor who is prepared to take on higher risk to obtain a high expected return will borrow at rate F and invest in portfolio M. This portfolio will therefore lie along the segment MZ. Similarly, an investor who has a strong dislike of risk will have a portfolio along the segment FM.

Although portfolios other than M can be invested in, for example portfolio P, giving the line FPQ, these are sub-optimum as they give lower expected returns for all levels of risk. The capital market line FMZ says that returns on portfolios along it (i.e. efficient portfolios) are linearly related to the risk borne (as measured by the standard deviation of their returns). The expected return on a portfolio is given by the risk-free rate plus the risk borne multiplied by the slope of the C.M.L. The slope of the C.M.L. (called the price of risk) gives the additional expected return for each additional unit of risk.

The expected return on a portfolio is given by the following expression:

$$E(R_P) = R_F + \frac{[E(R_M) - R_F]\sigma_P}{\sigma_M} \tag{5.1}$$

where $E(R_P)$ = expected return on portfolio P, R_F = risk-free interest rate, $E(R_M)$ = expected return on the market portfolio M,

σ_P = standard deviation of returns on portfolio P, σ_M = standard deviation of returns on the market portfolio M.

Although the capital market line holds for efficient portfolios, it does not describe the relationship between the expected returns on individual securities, or inefficient portfolios, and their standard deviations. Instead the C.A.P.M. says the expected returns are given by the expression

$$E(R_j) = R_F + B_j[E(R_M) - R_F], \tag{5.2}$$

where $E(R_j)$ = expected return on security j, R_F = risk-free interest rate, $E(R_M)$ = expected return on the market portfolio M, B_j = the covariability of security j's returns to those of the market portfolio M, i.e. Cov $(R_j, R_M)/(\sigma^2)R_M$ – this is known as 'systematic risk'.

Thus the expected return on security (or portfolio) j is given by the risk-free rate F plus a constant multiplied by the expected return on the market portfolio. The constant is B_j, the systematic relationship that exists between the movement of a particular security's returns and the return on the market portfolio. The generally used measure of total risk for a security or portfolio is its standard deviation. When combining securities into a portfolio the expected return on the portfolio is the weighted average of expected returns of the individual securities. However, the variance (the square of the standard deviation) of the portfolio is not the weighted average of the individual security variances. Instead the variance of the portfolio is measured by the degree to which the individual securities returns covary. The covariance of an individual security is deemed to be given by its covariance with the market index;[5] this is known as 'beta'. Portfolio variance is represented by the weighted average of the covariances of the individual security returns with the market index. As an example, if a security's historical returns had been very variable, then this would be considered a traditionally risky investment. If, however, the security's price tended to go up when the market index went down, and vice versa, then the security's covariance becomes negative (beta becomes negative) and this reduces portfolio risk. In practice very few, if any, securities will have negative betas but some have very low positive betas and these will probably add little to a portfolio's variance but will contribute to its expected return. The main point of this discussion is that beta is the appropriate measure of risk of a security for portfolio purposes and in capital market theory it is only beta (and not the standard deviation of returns) which is rewarded by increased expected returns. The importance of beta is that it represents that part of risk that cannot be diversified away (by acquiring more securities). Additionally, no reward in the form of expected returns is given for that part of a share's price variability that is not explained by beta as this can be eliminated by increasing portfolio diversification.

Expressions (5.1) and (5.2) are similar except that risk is measured by the standard deviation in returns in equation (5.1) whilst risk in equation (5.2) is measured by beta. For efficient portfolios the two equations are equivalent – their returns are linearly related to both standard deviation and beta. Figure 5.2 shows the relationship in

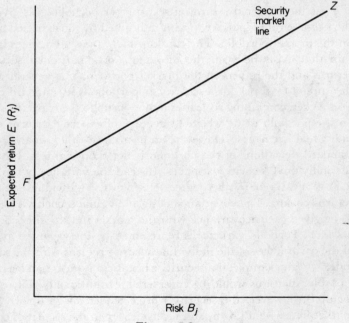

Figure 5.2

graphical form. The line $F\mathcal{Z}$ is known as the security market line (S.M.L.). (Note that the risk parameter is B_j in Figure 5.2 and not σ_j.) The S.M.L. can be used to calculate the expected return on an asset. Thus if $R_F = 5$ per cent, the expected return on the market was 12 per cent and the B for security j was 1·5, then the expected return on that security would be

$$E(R_j) = 5 \text{ per cent} + 1\cdot5(12 \text{ per cent} - 5 \text{ per cent})$$
$$E(R_j) = 15\cdot5 \text{ per cent.}$$

The major implications of the capital market line and the security market lines respectively are the following:

(1) that the rates of return on efficient portfolios are linearly related to total risk (either standard deviation or beta);

(2) that the rates of return on individual securities (or inefficient portfolios) are a linear function of systematic risk (beta). Given stability of the risk measures investors can derive conditional probabilities of expected returns. This in turn can lead to an investment decision-making process if the investor has confident views on the movement of the market index.

Use of the C.A.P.M. and the Market Model in Efficient-Markets Research

As the capital asset pricing model has provided the most acceptable theory relating to the pricing of individual securities it has been used in the efficient-markets research discussed in Chapter 7. A major segment of the efficient-markets research has sought to measure the impact of the announcement of some fundamental news on share prices. This is taken as the difference between the actual share price after the release of the news and the expected share price given no news. The expected price is given by the C.A.P.M. or its close relation, the market model. The market model is similar although not the same as the C.A.P.M. It measures the movement of security price returns as a function of movements in the market index. Thus:

$$R_j = a_j + B_j R_M + e_j \tag{5.3}$$

where R_j = rate of return on security j, R_M = rate of return on the market portfolio M, a_j and B_j are parameters that vary from security to security. B_j represents the covariance between the returns on security j and the returns on the market portfolio M. It is therefore the systematic risk of security j. e_j is a random variable whose expected value is zero.

The expected returns generated by the C.A.P.M. and the market model are used to derive the 'expected' prices in the efficient-markets research (see p. 128 for descriptions of this type of research). Additionally, the C.A.P.M. has been used to test portfolio performance, another popular type of research study used in the efficient-markets investigations (see p. 136). Because of the importance that the C.A.P.M. and the market model have in research studies, there is an obvious need to test and verify the validity of the models and especially their stability for the research periods covered.

The Validity of C.A.P.M. Assumptions

This section briefly evaluates the assumptions involved with the C.A.P.M. in light of real-world conditions and considers the impact of relaxing these assumptions on the validity of the model.

First, the risk-averse assumption does seem to hold. This can be evidenced by the large number of investors who choose to hold portfolios of securities as opposed to a single security.

The second assumption of identical time horizons and homogeneous expectations is clearly violated in the real world. First, investors clearly have different investment time horizons. More importantly, however, investors do not have identical expectations of returns and covariances. This will lead to investors having different efficient frontiers (see Figure 5.1) and hence there will be no one over-all C.M.L. or S.M.L. Thus portfolios which are efficient for one investor need not be efficient for another.

The assumption that the lending rate and the borrowing rate are the same and that they are the same for all investors is clearly unrealistic. The rate of interest earned on investing in a risk-free asset (probably a Government-backed security) is less than the interest rate that an investor would have to pay on borrowing monies to purchase 'risky' securities. The impact of this real-world situation can be seen in Figure 5.3. The lending rate is L and the borrowing rate is B and these touch the efficient frontier at different tangential points. The C.M.L., containing efficient portfolios, is now $LXYD$ and is no longer linear. Additionally, there is no one 'efficient portfolio' but a series of them making up the boundary XY. Thus an investor has the following alternatives open to him:

(1) lend at rate L;

(2) lend part of his funds at rate L and invest the remainder in portfolio X;

(3) invest all his funds in any portfolio along the curve XY;

(4) borrow money and together with his own funds invest in portfolio Y.

Equally unrealistic is that all investors have the same borrowing rates; some investors have better credit standing and thus are able to borrow at slightly lower rates than other investors. Thus the slope of the line BD varies between investors. Additionally, the rate of interest paid on borrowed monies is likely to vary in relation to the amounts borrowed, and hence the line YD is likely to be curvilinear rather than linear. The impact of relaxing the assumption is that we now have more than one C.M.L. and more than one S.M.L.

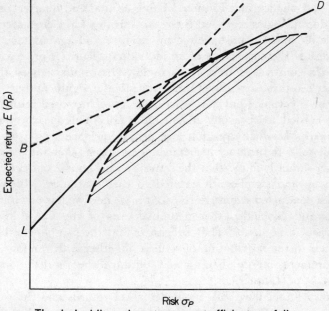

The dashed lines do not represent efficient portfolios

Figure 5.3

The assumption that there are no taxes and no transaction costs is also invalid in practice. Investors are interested in after-tax returns and differences will appear in the efficient frontiers faced by tax-exempt (for example pension funds) and tax-paying investors. The impact of both costs and taxes is to create different C.M.L.s and S.M.L.s for individual investors.

Empirical Tests of the Capital Asset Pricing Model

Although most of the assumptions involved in the C.A.P.M. are unrealistic we have not yet considered how much impact relaxing these assumptions has on the validity of the model. We can measure this impact, however, by conducting empirical tests into the explanatory and predictive powers of the model. Extensive tests of the validity of the C.A.P.M. have been made in the United States and although the results are somewhat woolly there has been no firm rebuttal of the model.

Amongst the first studies into the validity of the C.A.P.M. were those by Douglas[6] and Lintner.[7] Using annual and quarterly share price data Douglas regressed the returns from a large cross-sectional sample of shares against their own variance and against their own beta terms (the covariance of an individual security's price against an index constructed from the sample). His results showed that a security's return is positively and statistically significantly related to its own variance but not to its beta. Thus increased returns are being earned for bearing unsystematic risk. This clearly violates the C.A.P.M. which says that a security's variance should have no impact on its return once its beta value has been taken into account. Lintner similarly found that the returns on his sample of stocks were positively and significantly related to their variance. Miller and Scholes conducted extensive research into the Douglas and Lintner results and concluded that definitive tests of the C.A.P.M. still remained to be done.[8] They suggested that the combined effect of skewness in the distribution of returns, together with random error measurements in the beta, could produce the results found by Douglas and Lintner.

Arditti found that both realised market returns and the returns from a sample of thirty-four mutual funds were positively skewed, with mutual funds having a greater amount of positive skewness.[9] This led him to conclude that fund managers are willing to give up some expected return or take on more variability in exchange for a greater chance of earning a large return. Miller and Scholes found that the introduction of skewness in the C.A.P.M. leads to the beta coefficient being overstated and the residual variance being understated.[10] Kraus and Litzenberger added a measure of systematic skewness to the C.A.P.M.[11] Their new 'C.A.P.M.' model was tested on twenty portfolios consisting of securities on the New York stock exchange over a thirty-two year period. The authors found systematic skewness is a statistically significant explanatory factor of returns. Thus the expected return on securities is a function of both systematic risk and systematic skewness.

The next major piece of research into the validity of the C.A.P.M. was that by Black, Jensen and Scholes.[12] Their research found that low beta securities earned higher returns than expected and that high betas earned lower returns than expected.[13] In contrast McDonald, in a study of mutual fund performance in the period 1960–69, found that high beta portfolios tended to earn higher returns than expected – this, however, was not statistically significant.[14] The major implication of the Black–Jensen–Scholes research is that during the period they covered (1926–66) superior rates of return could have been earned for any given level of risk by purchasing low beta (low systematic risk) stocks and borrowing or lending to achieve the desired level of risk.

If the assumption of riskless lending and borrowing is relaxed, Black, Jensen and Scholes found that expected returns on securities were better explained by a two-factor model of the following form:[15]

$$E(R_i) = E(R_z)(1 - B_i) + E(R_M)B_i, \qquad (5.4)$$

where R_z = a portfolio that has no covariance (i.e. zero beta) with the market portfolio. It also has the lowest variance of all portfolios that have no correlation with the market. R_z is known as the 'beta factor'. The other factors are as before (see equation (5.2)).

The most recent study into the validity of the C.A.P.M. is that by Fama and MacBeth.[16] They used a linear regression model which involved regressing portfolio returns against three independent variables. These independent variables were

(1) the average of the betas calculated for each security in the portfolio using the market model;

(2) the average of the square of beta for each security in the portfolio; and

(3) the average standard deviation of the least-squares residuals from the market model for each security.

They tested their model on twenty portfolios of stocks registered on the New York stock exchange over the period January 1935 to June 1968. Various sub-periods between 1935 and 1968 were also examined.

Using the model the authors tested a number of hypotheses:

(1) that there is a linear relationship between expected return on a security and its risk in an efficient portfolio;

(2) that the systematic risk, beta, provides a complete measure of the risk of a security in an efficient portfolio;

(3) that higher risk is associated with higher returns; and

(4) that Sharpe's capital asset pricing model holds.

Fama and Macbeth were unable to reject the first three hypotheses but the fourth left some doubt. The authors found that the model of Black, Jensen and Scholes (see p. 97) provided a somewhat better description of expected returns.

Studies on mutual fund performance such as those by Sharpe,[17] Jensen,[18] Friend, Blume and Crockett,[19] the Institutional Investor Study, SEC,[20] and McDonald[21] found that higher returns are associated with increased systematic risk, this being in accordance with the C.A.P.M. The present author's study on U.K. unit trusts also found higher returns to be associated with higher levels of systematic risk.[22]

THE STABILITY OF BETA

A major practical consideration of the C.A.P.M. for investors is whether the systematic risk, beta, is stable over time. If it is relatively stable, then conditional expectations of future returns on portfolios and individual securities can be made.

An initial consideration is which data to use in constructing betas. Specifically, (1) should betas be derived from daily, weekly or other period price and market index recordings, and (2) how many recordings should be used, for example weekly recordings for one year? Although there has been some controversy over estimating betas,[23] Fisher found that the differences between the values of betas given by the various bases were slight.[24]

A number of researchers have turned their attentions to examining the stability of betas for both portfolios and individual securities over time. All found some instability, i.e. that betas changed across time, with individual security betas being more unstable than those

for portfolios. The conclusions of these researchers about whether
the betas were considered 'reasonably stable' or 'unstable' have
differed however. Jacob in an early study suggested that betas were
relatively unstable.[25] Blume studied the stability of betas for both
individual stocks and portfolios of stocks over consecutive seven-
year periods.[26] For individual securities the correlation coefficient
between successive seven-year period betas averaged about 0·6. In
contrast the correlation coefficient of ten stock portfolios was 0·9.
Blume also found a mean regressive tendency for beta values; this
means that if a beta departs from its average value, the next value
for beta will be such to bring it towards its average value again.
(Using this characteristic Blume was able to make improved predictions of future betas.) Levy found similar results as Blume with the
correlation coefficient ranging from below 0·5 for successive beta
values for individual securities to 0·85 for ten stock portfolios.[27]

Sharpe and Cooper conducted a later and much more extensive
study of the stability of individual security betas.[28] They classified
beta values by deciles and examined whether these shifted into
different decile classes over time. The proportion of security betas
that stayed in the same decile class varied from 0·75 to 0·35 after
one year and from 0·4 to 0·13 after five years. Sharpe and Cooper
also presented analyses which showed the proportions of betas that
remained within one decile class (i.e. did not move by more than
one decile) over time. The proportion of betas which remained
within one decile varied from 0·93 to 0·78 after one year and from
0·69 to 0·39 after five years. The authors concluded by interpreting
their results as suggesting that 'there is substantial stability over
time, even at the level of individual securities'. Other researchers,
however, have examined beta stability and reached differing conclusions – that betas were relatively unstable.[29] In addition some
researchers have developed theoretical models which have implied
that betas will not be stationary through time.[30] Cunningham has
examined the stability of betas of U.K. stocks.[31] He calculated the
correlation over 950 stocks between the betas in the period 1965–7
and the betas in 1968–70. The correlation coefficient came to 0·853
(when measuring betas using percentage changes in security returns
and the market index). He concluded that betas showed a marked
degree of persistence and that reasonable forecasts of future betas
can be made.

The above research studies have shown that portfolio betas are relatively stable whilst those for individual securities are much less so. Portfolio betas are more stable because individual security betas change upwards or downwards (in value) over time, and when these securities are combined into portfolios their changes tend to cancel each other out (well-selected portfolios with as little as ten stocks have been found to provide most of the diversification possible in portfolios).[32] The importance of the stability of beta for individual stocks is not so great for larger portfolios; however, it is important for investors who have very few shares in their portfolios or who choose to hold inefficient portfolios. If betas for individual securities change substantially over time, then an investor with only a few shares in his portfolio will find it difficult to maintain a desired risk level. The stability of beta for individual securities is also of considerable importance to researchers who have used the market model and the C.A.P.M. extensively in their empirical studies. If the beta values are unstable over the time period investigated, this can lead to difficulties in interpreting the results and may even make them invalid.

The Association of Accounting Measures of Risk and Market Measures of Risk

A fair amount of research has been carried out into explaining the levels of beta that exist for individual stocks. This was partly with the aim of seeing if betas were predictable, especially in the light of the previous section, in which individual security betas were found to have a fair amount of instability over time. Specifically researchers have attempted to associate economic and accounting (i.e. using published accounts) measures of risk to market measures of risk, namely beta.

Most studies have related accounting data to systematic risk. Ball and Brown,[33] for example, found there to be an association between systematic risk, beta, and the covariability of earnings of individual firms to an aggregate level of corporate earnings* (for example an earnings or accounting 'beta'; the greater a firm's

---

* The parameters of the model being estimated from the regression equation:

$$I_{jt} = a_j + B_j M_t + U_{jt},$$

where I_{jt} = movement in security j's earnings in year t, M_t = an index of the movement in the earnings in year t of all firms in the market, U_{jt} = random term, a_j and B_j are the parameters specific to security j.

earnings variability to the market average, the greater the accounting beta).

Beaver, Kettler and Scholes examined the relationship between
stock market risk measures (beta) and various accounting measures
of risk.[34] The accounting measures considered in their study were
the following:

(1) Dividend pay-out;

(2) Growth in total assets;

(3) Financial leverage – this was defined as the ratio of liabilities
to total assets;

(4) Liquidity as measured by the current ratio;

(5) Total assets;

(6) Earnings' variability as measured by the standard deviation of
the earnings/share price ratio;

(7) Earnings' covariability with the market average – this was
termed the 'accounting beta' by the authors – it is derived from a
simple regression model of a security's earnings – price ratio against
a market average earnings–price ratio (similar to that in the
footnote, p. 100).

The research methodology involved computing cross-sectional
correlation coefficients between the seven accounting variables and
the systematic risk, beta, for 307 firms. The results are shown in
Table 5.1. Four correlation coefficients, those for pay-out, leverage,
earnings' variability and accounting beta were statistically significant with earnings' variability giving the highest degree of association. The coefficients of the variables for portfolios were larger than
for individual securities. Beaver, Kettler and Scholes concluded
from these results that accounting measures of risk were good
explanatory variables of stock market systematic risk and that
accounting data are incorporated in market prices.

The authors also investigated whether accounting measures of
risk could predict systematic risk. Accounting data from the first
period 1947–56 were used to predict beta values for the period
1957–65. These predictions were compared against a naive no-
change forecast (i.e. that the same beta value for 1947–56 would
exist in the period 1957–65). The accounting measures of risk
found to provide better estimates of future beta
forecast. Other researchers also found a fair de
between various accounting measures of risk a

Table 5.1

*Contemporaneous association between market-determined measure of risk
and seven accounting risk measures**

Variable	Period 1 (1947–56)		Period 2 (1957–65)	
	Individual level	Portfolio† level	Individual level	Portfolio† level
Pay-out	−0·49 (−0·50)	−0·79 (−0·77)	−0·29 (−0·24)	−0·50 (−0·45)
Growth	0·27 (0·23)	0·56 (0·51)	0·01 (0·03)	0·02 (0·07)
Leverage	0·23 (0·23)	0·41 (0·45)	0·22 (0·25)	0·48 (0·56)
Liquidity	−0·13 (−0·13)	−0·35 (−0·44)	0·05 (−0·01)	0·04 (−0·01)
Size	−0·06 (−0·07)	−0·09 (−0·13)	−0·16 (−0·16)	−0·30 (−0·30)
Earnings' variability	0·66 (0·58)	0·90 (0·77)	0·45 (0·36)	0·82 (0·62)
Accounting beta (B_i)	0·44 (0·39)	0·68 (0·67)	0·23 (0·23)	0·46 (0·46)

* Rank-correlation coefficients appear in top row, and product-moment correlations appear in parentheses in bottom row.

† The portfolio correlations are based upon sixty-one portfolios of five securities each.

although none attempted to ascertain the predictive ability of this association. Amongst these studies were those by Bildersee,[35] Logue and Merville,[36] Beaver and Manegold,[37] Breen and Lerner,[38] and Gonedes;[39] although the degree of association varied amongst these studies, most concluded that accounting risk measures were major explanatory variables.

Rosenberg and McKibben used both accounting data and the historical distribution of a security's returns to predict current betas and the unsystematic risk (i.e. that part of total risk not accounted for by beta).[40] They found that accounting measures provided a certain amount of explanatory and predictive ability.

Pettit and Westerfield also found that accounting measures of risk provided little explanatory power of betas above that provided by other financial factors.[41] Other studies into explaining the level of beta include those by Hamada and Lev and Kunitzky. Hamada found that a firm's leverage has a significant impact on its beta (the percentage of the variability in beta explained by leverage, R^2, amounted to around 21 to 24 per cent).[42] Lev and Kunitzky found that 'smoothing' accounting data (i.e. reducing their variability) reduced a firm's beta (i.e. its systematic risk).[43]

These studies have shown that market measures of systematic risk are associated with accounting measures of risk. This is intuitively appealing as the accounting measures represent fundamental factors which affect a firm's earnings distribution and its economic value. However, there is contention in the use of accounting data in explaining betas as some researchers have found that other financial data give better explanations. Apart from the Beaver, Kettler and Scholes study there have been no major investigations into whether accounting data can give superior forecasts of future betas – this remains an area where more research is needed.

Summary

The capital asset pricing model has given us a theory which specifies the expected returns from individual securities. It is based upon a number of assumptions most of which are not strictly valid in the real world. Many researchers have investigated the validity of the C.A.P.M. using empirical studies and these indirectly measure the impact of relaxing the various assumptions. The results of these studies have varied somewhat and hence differing conclusions reached. The latest studies of the C.A.P.M., however, appear to support the Black, Jensen and Scholes model, in which expected returns are a function of both the expected return on the market and the return on a portfolio which has zero covariance with the market portfolio. In addition, Fama and Macbeth in one of the most thorough of recent studies concluded: (1) there was a linear relationship between expected returns on a security and its risk in an efficient market; (2) systematic risk, beta (B), provides a complete measure of the risk of a security in an efficient market; (3) higher risk is associated with higher returns. The evidence, therefore, seems to broadly support the C.A.P.M. and that the Black, Jensen and Scholes 'version' provides the best explanation of security returns (the recent work of Kraus and Litzenberger has provided another C.A.P.M. model – this utilising systematic skewness).

In utilising betas for estimating future risk, investors need to know their stability over time. Whilst the betas of portfolios have been found to be relatively stable, the same cannot be said for individual securities. Thus an investor who holds just one security will find that estimating his future risk, based on beta, will be very tenuous.

A large body of research has investigated the association of accounting measures of risk (which represent managerial – economic measures of risk) and market-based measures of risk, namely beta. The various studies have shown that there is a considerable amount of association and this is intuitively appealing. However, some researchers have found that using other financial data has provided even better explanatory models. Unfortunately little research has been done into whether accounting measures of risk can be used to predict future betas; the major study on this aspect is by Beaver, Kettler and Scholes and they found there was some predictive ability – much more work needs to be done however.

The validity of the C.A.P.M. and the market model, and the stability of betas, have an important bearing on the methodology used in a large section of efficient-market studies. If the models are invalid or if betas are significantly unstable over shortish periods of time, then some of the efficient-market studies' conclusions may be spurious. Brenner conducted a study which tested the sensitivity of the results concerning the efficient-markets theory in reacting to items of information (see p. 128 for descriptions of this type of research) for five different forms of the market model (including the Black, Jensen and Scholes version).[44] He found that the differences in results between using the various models were relatively minor. Brenner concluded his study by suggesting that future efficient-markets studies should use various forms of the market model in their test procedures.

CHAPTER 6

The Efficient-Markets Theory

In Chapter 1 we reviewed the *raison d'être* of the stock market and especially its role in the setting of share prices. Academics and practising investors have sought to 'measure' the performance of the pricing mechanism and to apply a description to the market. The currently prevailing description is the efficient-markets theory (E.M.T.). The E.M.T. has gained a broad level of acceptance as a description of the major stock markets, notably the New York Stock Exchange, the American Stock Exchange (both of the United States) and the United Stock Exchange (United Kingdom); the description has also been applied to other well-regulated markets although there has been a lesser amount of empirical testing.

An efficient market has been defined as one where share prices always fully reflect available information on a firm.[1] Thus the efficient-markets model implies that the complete body of publicly available knowledge about a company's prospects is interpreted correctly in the share price – the arrival of new information is impounded almost instantaneously into the price.

Obviously an efficient market, as described above, is desirable in socio-economic terms as savings will be channelled into the most profitable investments and thus capital will be allocated in an optimum manner. The role of the stock market as described in Chapter 1 will be optimised and the 'perfect knowledge' requirement of a perfect market will have been achieved in large measure.

In practice no existing stock market is perfectly efficient in the terms described above. Major shortcomings include that the complete body of knowledge about a company's prospects is not publicly available, and that even if such information were available it is doubtful if it would be interpreted in a completely accurate fashion in the share price. These shortcomings can impinge quite seriously on the E.M.T. such that the theory could break down altogether. This, of course, gives academic research considerable scope to justify itself by attempting to measure the performance of the stock market and the relevance of the efficient-markets theory.

Chapter 7 discusses the academic research that has been conducted into the E.M.T. Basically the approaches have been under three main headings:

(*a*) investigating whether share prices are predictable by examining past share prices;

(*b*) examining whether share prices react correctly to new items of fundamental information that become available; and

(*c*) determining whether any investors appear to have gained and used superior information and whether any investors have earned above-average returns.

The results from the research have broadly shown that (*a*) share price changes are unpredictable, (*b*) prices do adjust correctly (however, apart from a few cases, this approach is incapable of determining whether prices adjust 'perfectly'), (*c*) there was no evidence to show that many investors made large and consistent above-average returns. This research, however, has not provided a direct test of whether security prices accurately reflect the meaning of publicly available information (apart from the few cases cited in (*b*) above). What items (*a*) and (*c*) above have tested is whether share prices are predictable either by mechanical means or by certain individuals. In an efficient market where prices always fully reflect available information one would expect that the next period's price change would be unpredictable (the price changes depending upon new items of fundamental information which are unpredictable as to their occurrence and content). Thus the unpredictability of share price returns is consistent with, but on its own not sufficient for, the efficient-markets theory.[2]

To many, the recent volatility of the major stock markets has had little to do with the economic valuation of business enterprises and that the stock markets have done a very poor job in allocating capital. They contend that the economic values of quoted firms have not changed by anywhere near comparative amounts as their share prices and that the stock market is not efficient in its pricing. This point of view has been emphasised by many U.K. company

officials in 1973–4 who have publicly stated that they have not gone
to the stock market for additional equity financing because their
firms' share prices were unrealistically low.

Unfortunately it is difficult to arrive at confident opinions
relating to the economic accuracy of share prices. This is because
share prices rely heavily on long-term growth-rate forecasts which
themselves are dependent upon uncertain economic, government
and social changes. It is virtually impossible to say whether these
long-term growth-rate forecasts were 'correctly' arrived at, at the
time. On the one hand the forces at work in the stock market (see
the next section) would appear to argue that prices are correctly
arrived at, whilst on the other the recent volatility of stock market
levels argues against a 'correct' pricing performance.

The argument being put forward here is that the research methodologies that have been applied in investigating the E.M.T. have not
been wholly sufficient to test its applicability. All that can be validly
concluded is that prices are set in a very competitive market; this is
consistent with, but not on its own sufficient for, market efficiency.
There appears to be no quantitative way in which the E.M.T. can be
adequately tested. All that can be done is to subjectively appraise
the processes at work in the stock market and then reach an opinion
as to its efficiency.

The Economic Rationale of the Efficient-Markets Theory

The efficient-markets theory is based upon there being a fair, well-
regulated, competitive market-place and upon rational, profit-
seeking investors. The protagonists of the efficient-markets theory
say that there are so many expert, competing analysts evaluating the
same basic data that they will bring a security's price to its correct
level or, as it is often called, its 'intrinsic value'. Any errors in prior
pricing performance are monitored and analysed by these analysts
and their techniques and investment appraisal are adjusted accordingly. The process of share price formation is therefore represented
by a dynamic equilibrium model – the weighted mean of all
investors' opinions at that point in time. When new information
relevant to a security is received this is evaluated immediately by
analysts and its impact incorporated in the share price almost
instantaneously. Any under and any over adjustment and the time
taken to adjust are randomly distributed and small in magnitude.

Thus shares priced in an efficient capital market are said to wander randomly around their intrinsic values. The fluctuation around the intrinsic value represents the initial reaction to new information and the changing uncertainty in the opinions of investors in re-evaluating past items of news. Thus the competing nature of investment analysis, along with the regulatory control over financial disclosure and the dealing mechanism, are necessary prerequisites for an efficient market. The remainder of this chapter will briefly review the competitive nature of investment analysis and the regulatory influences on the market in the United Kingdom.

The major elements in reaching a highly competitive marketplace are the following:

(1) the existence of many highly trained investment analysts specialising in certain sectors of securities;

(2) the disclosure of relevant economic information by firms relating to their performance and their prospects, this disclosure being equally available to all investors; and

(3) the existence and exercise of regulatory control over investment dealing such that no one set of individuals or investors has an advantage over others.

(1)   THE INVESTMENT ANALYST PROFESSION

The major stockbrokers and investment institutions in the United Kingdom employ many highly trained investment analysts who specialise in specific shares. Typically analysts specialise in the larger companies in a specific industry. For example, an analyst may well continuously monitor the performance of the ten major property companies and undertake less regular reviews of the smaller property companies. Table 6.1, derived from an article by Braham,[3] shows the number of analysts employed by some of the major stockbroking firms in 1972. This number has been enhanced considerably since that date and in addition it only covers twenty-eight stockbrokers with no institutions being included. The Society of Investment Analysts, the professional body representing investment analysts, has a membership of over 1700, and this compares with the fact that there are over 3000 companies quoted on the U.K. stock exchange. This suggests that there are a fair number of investment analysts specialising in identical shares.

Although there are no formal examination requirements for an individual to become an analyst, most are in fact highly trained

Table 6.1

Stockbrokers' investment research departments

Broker	Number of analysts	Specialities
James Capel	40	Food, food processing, stores, breweries, oils, chemicals, financials, electricals, communications, engineering, building, paper and packaging, mining
Capel-Cure Carden	7	Retailing, textiles, paper, catering, entertainment, hotels, building materials
W. I. Carr	10	Mining, T.V. contractors and rentals, financial, stores, food manufacturing and retailing, building and contracting, textiles, shipping, breweries, catering, Far East
de Zoete & Bevan	16	Tobacco, food manufacturing, retailing, building and building materials, financial (esp. discount houses), hotels, T.V. rental, electricals, breweries, convertibles
Fielding Newson-Smith	9	Light electricals, oils, financials (esp. banks), mines, breweries, textiles
Panmure Gordon	18	Breweries, hotels, catering, H.P., banks, composite insurance, electricals, stores, tobacco, engineering, motors
W. Greenwell	30	Banks, insurance, oils, building materials, electricals, electronics, entertainment, motor components, mines, gilts
Grieveson Grant	20	None
Hedderwick Borthwick	9	Hotels, T.V. contractors and rentals, oils, holiday camps, shipping, financial, building
George Henderson	8	Mining (esp. S. Africa), oils, stores, breweries, engineering, financial

Table 6.1 *continued*

Stockbrokers' investment research departments

Broker	Number of analysts	Specialities
Hoare & Co. Govett	35	Boilermakers, breweries, bricks, cement, chemicals, domestic appliances, heavy electricals, carpets, furniture, textiles, H.P., hotels and catering, machine tools, milling and baking, motors, newspapers, office equipment, oils, paper, board and packaging, pharmaceuticals, plastics and rubber, processed foods, pumps and valves, shipping, shipbuilding, steel and chemical plant, multiple stores, tobacco, mines
Hoblyn Dix Maurice & Anderson	8	H.P., hotels
Kitcat & Aitken	20	Oil, paper, investment trusts, insurance composites and brokers, retailing, shipping, tobacco, Eurodollars, convertibles, N. America, Europe, Australasia
Laing & Cruickshank	10	Property, mining (esp. S. Africa), food, stores, textiles, chemicals, pharmaceuticals, engineering, paper, building
Laurence Prust	10	Food, oils, carpets, Australians, rubbers, tins, motor components, investment trusts, aerospace, T.V. rentals, breweries, mines, electricals, greeting-card manufacturers, laundries, warrants
Laurie Milbank	6	Stores, foods, banking, H.P., electricals, paper and packaging, building, motors
L. Messel	25	None
Mitton Butler Priest	15	Building and construction, mining finance

Broker	Number of analysts	Specialities
Myers	10	Investment trusts, mining (esp. Australia), property, stores, consumer non-durables
Norris Oakley Richardson & Glover	10	Investment trusts, hotels, property, steel stockholders, independent steel companies, Hong Kong
Phillips & Drew	12	None
Rowe & Pitman	25	Electricals, oils, mining finance, property, gilts, fixed interest, U.S. West Coast
E. B. Savory Milln	15	Insurance, engineering, building, European arbitrage, S. Africa
J. & A. Scrimgeour	8	Oils, property, motors, engineering, chemicals, building, retailing
Joseph Sebag	20	Retailing, composite insurance, banks, property
Sheppards & Chase	15	Banks, breweries, insurance brokers, chemicals, food distribution, retailing, paper
Simon & Coates	30	None
Vickers da Costa	20	Japan, Europe, S. Africa

people. Typically, analysts are graduates and many have a professional qualification, the major ones being in accountancy or actuarial work. The graduates are from various disciplines, although there is a strong trend towards those having done business studies; many of these degrees contain a unit in investments. Many analysts have had prior experience in the sector in which they specialise, for example chartered surveyors becoming property share analysts, chemists specialising in chemical shares, accountants and business graduates specialising in an industry in which they once worked as an executive. Stockbroking firms and investment institutions tend to be located in a few centres, the major one in the United Kingdom being London of course. This has meant that investment analysts have changed jobs more than might have been expected and has also enabled greater personal contact between analysts to be built up. All this has created a greater exchange of information between analysts both as regards investment techniques and as regards specific company evaluation. Analysts can often get hold of the formal reports prepared by rival analysts. Whilst this is usually done secretly it certainly does exist. As a concluding point, investment analysts are comparatively highly paid, which again helps attract high calibre personnel!

The above has briefly reasoned that U.K. share prices are being evaluated by many highly expert personnel. In fact there is reason to believe that there are too many investment analysts working on the major shares, given the existing disclosure levels of economic information. In Braham's article cited above, there was a quote from the senior research analyst of a firm of stockbrokers which was as follows: 'It means that everyone is working on the same few hundred major groups and there is serious overproduction of research material on them.' Similar comments have been made in the United States. For example, Wallich has said:

> Incorrect pricing can produce serious disturbance. Here is the main social contribution of securities analysis. But approximately correct pricing could probably be obtained with a fraction of the manpower now employed in securities analysis. Once the best available judgement has put prices where they belong, there is no social benefit in duplicating the work ... correct pricing of securities ... is a public good available free to all, even though it costs money to produce. Anybody can get the benefit of the combined best judgement by simply accepting the prices set by the market.[4]

There are opposing views of course who say that if society is prepared to 'pay' for analysts' advice then they must be useful. For example, Rinfret has said: 'In the market economy we live in, the ultimate test of anything is what the market will pay. The market pays for investment advice because investment advice is worth paying for';[5] and the large number of investment services gives some credence to Rinfret's remarks.

(2) THE DISCLOSURE OF FINANCIAL INFORMATION

There are various rules and regulations relating to the disclosure of financial information by companies. These have been designed so as to give as much relevant information to investors as is possible without giving away detailed knowledge to competitors, and to ensure that the information is equally available to all investors. The *Companies Acts* of 1948 and 1967 lay down provisions relating to the form and content of annual reports, which constitute the major single information source used by analysts. The *Acts* do not, however, say much about the accounting policies to be adopted. This is partly made up for by the accounting bodies themselves, which lay down standards in financial reporting – these have the effect of making accounting information more consistent over time and more comparable between different firms. The major accounting bodies have joined forces to create what is known as the Accounting Standards Committee (A.S.C.), the function of which is to create standards in financial reporting to which limited companies are expected to comply. Although there is room for considerable improvement in the form and content of annual accounting information,[6] the existing state has still enabled investors to obtain a large amount of useful data therefrom. The stock exchange has also laid down regulations relating to the reporting of economic information by firms. For example, it is the stock exchange who require that quoted companies must issue half-yearly reports. Although these are usually unaudited they do provide information on sales, profits and dividends which is of significant help to the analyst.

Apart from the above legal or quasi-legal regulations relating to disclosure there exist a large number of private firms who provide economic and financial statistics relating to quoted companies. The two most well-known statistical services are those run by Extel and Moodies. These provide a wide array of information on companies and industries for a smallish fee. There are many other sources of economic information and investment advice which are available for subscription. Most investors also make use of the numerous financial papers and journals which contain a lot of information and opinion. In summary there exists a host of economic information and investment comment which, for small fees, are available to investors and analysts.

(3) — THE REGULATORY CONTROL OVER THE MARKET

It is essential that any undesirable dealing practices which arise should be dealt with quickly and firmly. If this does not happen, then the undesirable practices will rapidly expand and so the market will gain a very speculative flavour. This will of course deter the vast majority of private individuals from directly or indirectly investing in equity shares. The major forms of undesirable practices which have occurred in the past include the issuing of misleading statements by the directors of a company, and insider dealing. The issuing of misleading or incorrect financial statements include those which constitute an offer of shares for sale and those which involve the publication of annual accounts. Nowadays the scope for issuing deliberately misleading financial statements has been much reduced as independent bodies are involved in vetting the statements, i.e. independent auditors in the case of annual accounts, and the reporting accountants and the issuing house in the case of prospectuses. Additionally, the *Companies Acts* impose fairly heavy penalties on directors who are found guilty of issuing misleading and false financial statements.

Insider dealing, however, has been more difficult to identify and eradicate. Insider dealing consists of a person(s) who has obtained non-publicly available information on a company because of his position (i.e. a director, senior-management employee, auditor, financial adviser) and uses this to make investment gains. The stock exchange, the Takeover Panel and the Departments of Trade and Industry have powers to investigate share deals when there is a strong suspicion of insider dealing. The stock exchange has strong powers because its ultimate threat is to cancel the quotation of a company if it continues to be a source of leaks and if it refuses to co-operate in any official stock exchange investigation. The Takeover Panel was set up in the late 1960s by the major City of London financial institutions. The Panel's particular powers lay in investigating share dealings around the time of takeovers and mergers – this of course being a time of substantial share price movements and hence presents considerable scope for insider-dealing profits to be made.

In exceptional cases the Departments of Trade and Industry may be called to investigate investment-dealing matters. Occasionally this has led to criminal proceedings being brought against directors, officers of the company and others involved in issuing misleading financial statements or in share dealing malpractices.

Whilst these bodies have helped deter undesirable investment practices there still remains a certain amount of scope for insiders to profit from their knowledge. The use of nominee names or buying shares through a friend's name is quite common practice, and as long as the amounts involved are not large, share prices will not react unexpectedly (which would normally call for a stock exchange investigation) and thus no strong evidence of insider dealing comes to light. It would appear that, in general, the amounts involved in insider dealing are not too large and thus the U.K. stock market's competitiveness has not been affected greatly.

The above paragraphs have described the competitive and regulated nature of the United Stock Exchange. Clearly the U.K. stock market is fairly sophisticated in this regard and this has been evidenced by the large numbers of individuals who continue to directly and indirectly invest in equity investments. (Smaller market capitalisation firms are less intensively analysed by the market professionals and the number of shares 'on the market' is far less – this creates a position where market efficiency for these shares is reduced. See the reference to Girmes and Benjamin's study on p. 125.)[7] Improvements can of course be made both to improve the existing situation and to adjust for any change in the circumstances surrounding the investment environment.

A similar competitive, well-regulated market-place also exists in the United States. There are around 11,000 professional investment analysts in the United States working for stockbrokers and financial institutions. The Stock Exchange (the New York Stock Exchange, N.Y.S.E., and the American Stock Exchange AMEX, are the two major American exchanges) and the Securities and Exchange Commission (S.E.C.) both lay down regulations as to the dealing mechanism and investment behaviour. Additionally, they both require fairly substantial amounts of financial disclosure by companies. The American Institute of Certified Public Accountants (A.I.C.P.A.) have produced recommended accounting practices which the quoted companies are expected to adhere to. The A.I.C.P.A. have also set up a Financial Accounting Standards Board (F.A.S.B.) which is responsible for setting accounting standards (a similar function to the A.S.C. in the United Kingdom).

The Securities and Exchange Commission (S.E.C.) was established by the *Federal Securities Act* of 1933 and its powers extended by the *Securities Exchange Act* of 1934. The S.E.C. exercises considerable powers over the American investment scene; specifically:

(1) it requires disclosure of certain items of financial information, and in particular formats, from quoted companies;

(2) it requires disclosure of certain share dealing activities (for example transactions by an officer in the shares of his employer company);

(3) it can investigate any suspected malpractice by companies (for example issuing misleading information) or by investors;

(4) it can suspend a firm's quotation; and

(5) it publishes statistics and commentaries on various investment matters.

The U.S. investment setting is in fact probably more sophisticated than that in the United Kingdom and this is often attributed to the impact of the S.E.C. A number of people have thus advocated the setting up of a S.E.C. in the United Kingdom. Whilst this has not been taken up yet, it remains a possible development, especially if the stock exchange fails to inspire confidence in its regulatory mechanisms. Other major stock markets of the world also have fairly extensive regulatory control exercised over them so as to prevent abuse.

Summary

This chapter has briefly described the efficient-markets theory. Whilst its economic rationale is plausible, it is contended that the E.M.T. is probably impossible to prove. The empirical testing of the theory has produced results consistent with market efficiency but one must apply subjective judgement to these in order to reach conclusions on the validity of the E.M.T. The results in fact suggest a 'competitive market hypothesis', i.e. one where there is a good deal of competition such that it is difficult to obtain above-average investment returns by 'fair' means. A competitive market is a prerequisite for an efficient market. Chapter 7 summarises some of the major research studies testing the E.M.T. and Chapter 8 discusses the implications of the E.M.T. for accounting.

Tests of the Efficient-Markets Theory

Given that the stock market exerts considerable influence on the economy it is obviously important that its performance should be measured, and specifically that the efficient-markets theory (E.M.T.) be tested. Until the early 1960s, however, very few quantitative studies had been made into share price behaviour and hence little was known about the efficiency of the market. Since that date there has been an enormous, almost explosive, growth in research in the United States, this being largely occasioned by the construction of computerised data banks which store share price information and accounting information in an easily accessible form. This has enabled statistical analyses to be run and has enabled various plausible investment rules to be evaluated over long time periods. The major data banks are the C.R.I.S.P. (Centre for Research into Security Prices) tapes, compiled originally at Chicago University, Compustat tapes and the tapes maintained by Wells Fargo Bank.

It is only recently that comparable data banks have been developed in the United Kingdom (notably those at the London Graduate School of Business Studies and at City University), and hence only a small amount of efficient-markets research has been conducted in the United Kingdom. This means of course that the E.M.T. as it relates to the U.K. stock market has been largely untested; there is no reason why the results of the American studies should be automatically imputed for other stock markets. The evidence described in this chapter relates mainly to the United States and readers should recognise this when making implications relating to the United Kingdom. Whilst many people are prepared to argue that the U.K. stock market is efficient, because of American research, these are only subjective opinions (research in the United Kingdom has produced results similar to those in the United States)

Research studies into share price behaviour (a term used synonymously with efficient-market studies) have been conducted by two distinct groups. One has been practising investment advisers who have attempted to derive successful investment techniques. If the technique is only mildly successful (in terms of outperforming the market), or if it no longer works, then the adviser may decide to publish the results and hence they are added to the E.M.T. literature. They probably publish their findings either to show how good their advice is or as a life story of how they earned their fortune. It seems unlikely that any existing consistently profitable investment strategy would be published by an analyst as this would be discounted away by the market. This means of course that successful investment strategies are 'unknown' to the academic community and hence no research has been conducted into them. The second major group of researchers have been academics who are interested in determining the influences at work in the stock market. In the majority of cases the academic studies have been statistically sounder than those undertaken by practising analysts. Many academic researchers have in fact investigated 'successful' investment rules promulgated by practising analysts – as described earlier, however, we might expect these 'rules' to no longer work (why else should the analyst publish the rule?).

The empirical research is usually categorised into three main types, these being the following:

(*a*) *Weak-form tests* these have measured whether past recordings of share prices or other financial data can be used in a mechanical sense to predict future prices;

(*b*) *Semi-strong-form tests* these have attempted to test whether share prices accurately and instantaneously reflect all new public information pertaining to the security;

(*c*) *Strong-form tests* these have attempted to test whether there is much investment use made of inside information and whether any investors appear to have consistently superior success.

Research relating to these three forms of market efficiency, each in turn being a more stricter test of the E.M.T., is discussed below. Before commencing with this, however, a number of points need to be borne in mind. They are as follows.

(1) Although described as tests of the E.M.T. they are only

providing necessary evidence for or against the theory and do not constitute sufficient evidence, one way or the other (this point was emphasised earlier on p. 107).

(2) Few people argue that the market is perfectly efficient but many say that it is good enough to give it the general title of being efficient; thus a few minor inefficiencies are expected but these do not greatly disturb the stock market's function in allocating capital resources. Whilst this view is reasonable it does bring in the problem of deciding how much 'inefficiency' the E.M.T. can stand. There has been no research into measuring the full economic impact of a stock market's 'inefficiency' although this is probably an impossible task to do with precision anyway. The problem has in fact led different researchers to make opposite conclusions on market efficiency when faced with identical data. For example, in testing the weak form of the E.M.T. many researchers have measured the statistical dependence in successive price changes and virtually all have found some, very small, serial correlation. Some researchers have construed this to mean that the E.M.T. is refuted (taking a strict definition of market efficiency) whilst others have said the serial correlation is so small that no profitable trading rules can be based upon such dependence and hence the market is efficient.

(3) If inefficiencies are found and identified in published research, then they may, depending on their form, be discounted away. For example, if a profitable trading strategy is publicised, then investors will surely adopt it, such that the profit potential will be discounted away; thus Granger has remarked: 'One might say that the random walk model is inevitable – if there were any other rule operating, then there would exist sure-fire investment strategies which, if used by a sufficient number of investors (speculators?) would just as inevitably wipe out the successful rule.'[1] This represents a positive step that researchers can make in contributing to market efficiency, i.e. identifying inefficiency.

(4) The efficient-markets theory is an extreme null hypothesis and so formal tests of the model will go on and on. Additionally, the E.M.T. is partially the result of the conditions of the stock market at that point in time and thus continuing research is needed to see if the model is valid. This has already been acknowledged by many researchers whose studies are replications of earlier research but on new, current, data.

Tests of the Weak-Form Efficient-Markets Theory

These investigations have set out to establish whether past series of share prices can be used to successfully predict future share prices. The major analysis used in these studies has been to measure the statistical dependence between price changes. Thus the serial correlation (the correlation between a price change at day t and the price change recorded at day $t - 1$) between successive price changes of a security is measured. The period over which the price changes were measured have varied from one day to over ten days, all in an attempt to identify some form of dependence. Unfortunately research has shown that share price changes are not normally distributed and this implies that the normal serial-correlation techniques are not strictly valid for this data (a discussion of this problem is dealt with on p. 137). At this stage it is worth saying that many researchers believe that the results from the serial-correlation tests are still generally valid.

If no dependence is found (i.e. price changes are random), then this provides evidence in support of the E.M.T. as it signifies that no profitable investment trading strategy can be derived based on past prices; thus today's price is the best estimate of tomorrow's price. If dependence is found, for example a price increase is generally followed by a price increase in the next period, then clearly this can form the basis of a profitable investment rule. Whether the rule is profitable depends largely on the costs of operating it (brokerage costs and interest costs) and on whether transactions can be made at the exact prices quoted in the market.

These studies of statistical dependence in share prices are testing whether prices follow a random walk, and in the 1960s the efficient-markets literature was in fact known as the 'random-walk literature'. It is now generally argued that prices need not follow a strict random walk, that is zero correlation between successive price changes, for the E.M.T. to be valid. Only if the dependence is so great as to permit the existence of consistently profitable trading rules ·is the E.M.T. violated.

The first major study examining speculative prices in a competitive market was by Bachelier.[2] Working before the turn of the century he found that commodity prices on the French *Bourse* followed a random walk. After Bachelier's contribution research into share prices lagged somewhat. Further work by Working,[3] Cowles and Jones[4] in the United States and by Kendall[5] in the United

Kingdom also found evidence that security prices followed a random walk. Kendall's data consisted of the weekly changes in nineteen indices of U.K. industrial share prices. (Care has to be exercised in using serial-correlation analyses on indices. The first-order coefficient will be biased upwards if prices used to construct the index do not occur simultaneously (and this is often the case) – thus the index measures the average level over the period of price collection. Working has shown that the correlation of first differences of averages in a random chain can induce correlations not present in the original data and the coefficient will tend towards 0·25 as the number of periods averaged increases.)[6]

Two articles by Roberts and Osborne, both published in 1959, stimulated a great deal of discussion of the then named 'random-walk theory' and which, along with the construction of data banks, motivated a large growth in research into share price behaviour. Roberts's study compared the movements in the Dow Jones industrial average (a stock market average) with the movement in a variable which was generated from a random-walk process.[7] He found that the random-walk process produced patterns which were very similar to those of the Dow Jones index. This of course suggested that changes in the index are randomly distributed and hence cannot be predicted from past values of the index. Figure 7.1 shows the simulated market level and Figure 7.2 shows the actual levels of the Dow Jones industrial index. Figures 7.3 and 7.4 likewise show the patterns created by changes in the random numbers and changes in the index (the source of all four figures is Roberts's study). Clearly there is a good deal of similarity.

Osborne's study found a close resemblance between share price changes and the random movement of small particles suspended in a solution, which is known in physics as the 'Brownian motion'.[8] His study, like that of Roberts, had suggested that share price changes may be random in nature and that past prices had no predictive value.

During the 1960s there was an enormous growth in serial-correlation testing as various researchers made use of the newly established data banks. None of these has found any substantial linear dependence in price changes – however, as mentioned previously, what little dependence there was (and virtually all researchers have found some) has led to different conclusions being drawn on the E.M.T. by various researchers. Amongst the major

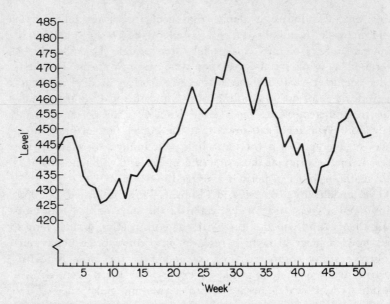

Figure 7.1 *Simulated market levels (random numbers) for fifty-two weeks*

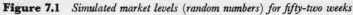

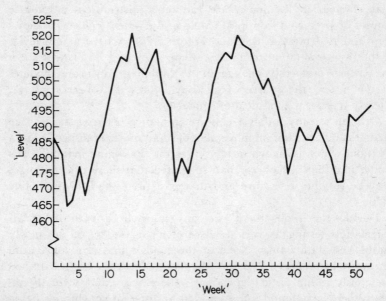

Figure 7.2 *Actual Friday closing levels, 30 December 1955–28 December 1956
(Dow Jones industrial index)*

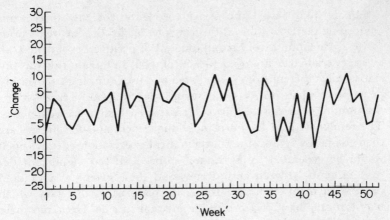

Figure 7.3   *Simulated market changes (random numbers) for fifty-two weeks*

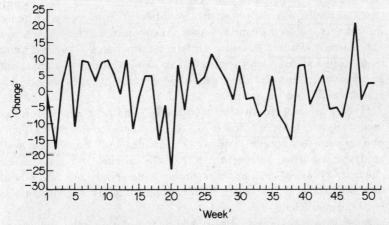

Figure 7.4   *Actual changes from Friday to Friday (closing levels), 6 January 1956–*
28 December 1956 (Dow Jones industrial index)

studies are those by Moore,[9] Fama[10] and Hagerman and Richmond.[11] Moore found an average serial-correlation coefficient of
−0·06 for price changes measured over weekly intervals. This
shows that there was a slight tendency for weekly price changes to
reverse, i.e. a price fall to follow a price rise and vice versa. The
association was so small, however, that the coefficient was not
statistically different from zero, and the returns obtained from
utilising the dependence would certainly be insufficient to cover
trading expenses.

Fama's study tested the serial correlation for the thirty firms comprising the Dow Jones industrial average for the five years prior to 1962. He found a very small amount of positive dependence (an average serial-correlation coefficient of 0·03) but again this was not statistically different from zero. Fama also used runs tests to measure dependency. This involves measuring the duration of runs, that is the duration of successive price increases or successive price decreases. The results of these for both individual stocks and for indices are then compared against the mathematical expectation of runs which would be generated by a random process. If any significant departure exists between actual runs and those given by a random process, then this indicates there are patterns in the data which may form the basis of a profitable investment rule. He found there was a slight tendency for price changes to be followed by price changes of the same sign (positive correlation) but this was so small that the results were not statistically different from zero and hence the changes followed a random walk. Many studies followed Moore's and Fama's work each using different data bases. The results of these studies were much the same as those of Moore and Fama, but as already mentioned the conclusions made by the various researchers differed somewhat.

Hagerman and Richmond conducted similar analyses but on securities which were traded in the 'over-the-counter' (O.T.C.) market. As this market consists of smaller and hence less well analysed securities, it might be that the market is therefore less efficient. However, the authors found little serial correlation and thus the market for even the smaller-type company appeared to be weak-form efficient.

Some researchers have also looked at the market efficiency in the pricing of 'other-type' equity securities. For example, Black and Scholes looked at the options market (options give the investor the right to sell at a specific price (a 'put') or buy at a specific price (a 'call') in a particular time period).[12] Whilst they found that there was significant mispricing of the options, this could not be used as the basis for a profitable trading rule because of the high transaction costs that would be incurred. Serial-correlation tests of dependence have also been carried out in various stock markets around the world, for example Praetz on Australian stocks,[13] and Brealey,[14] Cunningham[15] and Dryden[16] in the United Kingdom. These have similarly revealed little or no serial correlation. Praetz, Brealey and

Dryden also used runs tests in analysing their data and again there was no significant evidence of dependence. In a later study of the U.K. market, Girmes and Benjamin found evidence of non-randomness in the share price behaviour of small, lightly traded stocks.[17] This contrasted with their results for larger companies where share price changes were randomly distributed. The difference in the results may be due to the fact that the smaller firms are less intensively analysed in the stock market; this contrasts with Hagerman and Richmond's study which showed that the securities market for the smaller size U.S. companies was relatively efficient. In addition to the ordinary serial-correlation analyses, use has been made of spectral analysis. The basic assumption in this methodology is that values of one variable are known at times $t = 1, 2, 3 \ldots$ and a number of functions based on this series may be calculated and output. These may then be used as a basis for hypotheses regarding the actual structure of the time series. The major study using spectral analysis has been carried out by Granger and Morgenstern.[18] Their findings have been consistent with those described above, i.e. the serial correlation found was very small.

The testing of statistical dependence in price changes has received an enormous amount of research during the past decade. The results have been virtually unanimous in finding little or no statistical dependence and this has corroborated the weak-form efficient-market theory. (A few researchers have opposed these findings, for example Ying,[19] Cheng and Deets,[20] and Philippatos and Nawrocki.[21] However, the researchers did not show whether the dependencies they found could lead to profitable investment decisions after including costs. Additionally, the problems in definitions (see p. 119) may account for these opposing conclusions.)

A large body of research has also been directed towards testing whether mechanical investment strategies can earn above-average returns. These strategies give objective signals for buying and selling securities, and because they are so explicit they can be easily tested. Strictly speaking many successful mechanical strategies require there to be some dependence in price changes, and as described above there is little evidence of this – however, it may be that the pattern is very complex and thus indetectable by serial-correlation measures. Many of the investigations by academic researchers have in fact tested 'successful' investment strategies suggested and publicised by practising investment advisers. In the vast majority of cases the academic studies have found the strategies to be unprofitable and have instead suggested that there are no simple mechanical ways to consistently earn above-average returns. The reasons for the discrepancies between the results revealed by practising investment advisers and those of academics have been largely due to the following:

(i) The 'profitable' strategies being based upon statistically and economically spurious testing;

(ii) The 'profitable' rule only working on one set of historical data and not being of use on any other data. This of course means the rule cannot be used to generate profits in the future. For example, in testing and refuting the relative-strength investment criteria, Jensen and Bennington said:

> given enough computer time, we are sure that we can find a mechanical trading rule which 'works' on a table of random numbers – provided of course that we are allowed to test the rule on the same table of numbers which we used to discover the rule. We realise of course that the rule would prove useless on any other table of random numbers, and this is exactly the issue with Levy's results.[22]

Amongst the various investment strategies that have been tested are the following:

(i) *Filter-rules*. These provide buy and sell signals when share prices have moved a certain percentage away from a high or low point, for example if a price rises by at least x per cent, buy and hold the security until its price drops by at least x per cent from a subsequent high; when the price decreases x per cent or more, sell the securities until they rise by x per cent. Various values for x and various modifications to the rule have been proposed and tested. Whilst some researchers have found very small profits, these have all disappeared once transaction costs were included.

Amongst the major American studies investigating this rule were those by Alexander,[23] who originally advocated the filter strategy, and Fama and Blume,[24] who found that the returns were insufficient to meet the costs generated. Studies by Dryden[25] in the United Kingdom and Praetz[26] in Australia found that filter strategies did not achieve above-average returns.

(ii) *Moving averages*. This involves buying or selling shares as their prices move up or below their moving average. Researchers have used various periods over which to calculate the moving average and they have experimented with various action limits, for example buy if the share price moved 5 per cent above its moving average. Again no significantly profitable investment rule has been found to exist after allowing for transaction costs. Examples of research of this type include those by Cootner,[27] Van Horne and Parker[28] and James[29]

(iii) *Fixed-proportion maintenance strategies* whereby at the end of each period the portfolio is adjusted so that the proportions of total funds invested in specific securities remain the same as at the beginning. Work by Evans[30] and Latané and Young[31] showed this strategy did not outperform a simple buy and hold policy.

(iv) *Relative-strength tests*. These strategies involve ranking shares in terms of price performance over some period and investing in the top x per cent and disinvesting from the bottom y per cent. The premise behind this strategy is that good performance will tend more often than not to be repeated to some extent in the next period. Various modifications and various cut-off percentages have been advocated by its users. Despite its many protagonists,[32] the academic research to date has been unable to verify the claims of profitable investment. The major recent academic study in this area was that by Jensen and Bennington;[33] they replicated Levy's relative-strength rules and found that they did not work on future data (hence their remarks quoted on p. 126).

Many other plausible investment strategies have been subjected to statistically sound empirical testing, and these, as those above, have not been found to consistently outperform the market index. (There have of course been a number of dissenting studies.[34] Although there are various shortcomings in these researches there has been no comprehensive analysis of the impact of these. Additionally, the disclosure of these rules may now have been discounted away – if not, then this would imply inefficiency.) Indeed many of the strategies appear to have consistently underperformed the market index, especially when transaction costs were included in the analysis. The importance of this type of research is that it covers investment strategies which rely upon dependencies or patterns in prices which are far too complex to identify by serial-correlation methods; additionally, they have tested rules which have been claimed to be profitable. The results of these researchers have corroborated those testing for statistical dependence and thus the evidence to date has not refuted weak-form market efficiency. However, the point made above (p. 118) has to be borne in mind, i.e. that any currently profitable trading rule is likely to be kept secret by its inventor, and thus the only publicised 'successful' rules are those which are no longer profitable.

Tests of the Semi-Strong Form of the Efficient-Markets Theory

These tests attempt to establish whether share prices react precisely and quickly to new items of information. If prices do not react in this way, then this indicates that the market cannot correctly interpret economic events and that potential exists for some cleverer investors to make substantial returns.

The general methodology involved in these studies has been to take an economic event and measure its impact on the share price. This impact is then analysed to see if it is reasonable (as will be described below, the normative impact of some items can be precisely determined). The 'impact' is measured by taking the difference between the actual change in price and the change in price that would have prevailed had there been no such event. This latter figure has usually been derived from the market model suggested by Sharpe.[35]

The market model involves regressing share price returns against industry or market average returns. (The derivation of the parameters of this model were described on p. 93. The market model typically accounts for around 20–30 per cent of the variability in a security's return (i.e. $R^2 = 20$–30 per cent).) This gives us a risk factor, beta (called 'systematic risk'). Using beta we can estimate the expected change in price by the expression $B_j R_{Mt}$, where B_j is the beta value of security j and R_{Mt} is the actual change in the portfolio index in period t. Thus the expected price change is solely dependent on movement in the market index. (King[36] has shown that the market factor is the major influence on share prices in the United States. Similar conclusions for the United Kingdom were reached by Draper.)[37] The impact of any event (U_{jt}) is thus:

$$U_{jt} = R_{jt} - B_j R_{Mt},$$

where R_{jt} is the actual movement or return (i.e. including any cash dividends) in period t. Thus the impact of any event is measured whilst holding steady the influence of the market.

The research has been carried out on two major types of economic events.

(1) Events which have a precise impact. Examples include capitalisation issues and dividend payments (ex-dividend prices). These provide the soundest basis for research although unfortunately they are few in number.

(2) Events which do not have a precise impact but for which the general direction can be estimated fairly confidently. Examples include announcements of large investment holdings being built up in firms, large purchases and sales of stock, and earnings announcements. Thus if a firm announces a greater than expected profit, we would expect the share price to rise – however, we have no precise idea by how much the price ought to increase (unless we have a strong belief in a simple equity valuation model such as that presented on p. 21). All that can be done in such research is to see if the actual price reacts in the right direction and that the adjustment procedure is completed speedily. Any attempt to see if the amount of the actual impact is 'correct' is tenuous (as we do not have a 'correct' value to use as a yardstick) and few researchers have attempted to do so. Instead they just see if the U_{jt} (known as the 'residuals') are of the right sign (positive or negative) and possibly make a subjective assessment of whether the magnitude is about 'right'.

The methodology has generally proceeded by measuring the economic impact of an event over a number of companies ($j = 1$, ... n), that is cross-sectionally, in order to measure the average impact for a particular period, d. Thus the average U_t for any individual day is measured thus:

$$U_t = \frac{1}{n} \sum_{j=1}^{n} U_{jt}.$$

Researchers also usually like to know the cumulative impact of the residuals, and this has been measured in two ways. First, there is what has been termed the 'cumulative average residual approach', which assumes a portfolio in which the investment in each security

$(j = 1, \ldots n)$ is adjusted so that there is an equal dollar investment in each security at the start of each period. The cumulative average residuals are calculated thus:

$$CU_T = \sum_t^T U_t.$$

CU_T gives the cumulative deviations of the returns on the securities from their normal relationships to market movements. This approach was used by Fama, Fisher, Jensen and Roll in their study on stock splits.[38]

The second major approach has been the construction of what is known as the Abnormal Performance Index (A.P.I.). The A.P.I. is computed thus:

$$\text{A.P.I.} = \frac{1}{N} \sum_{j=1}^{N} \left(\prod_t^M (1 + U_{jt}) - 1 \right).$$

This measures the value of a sum of money invested in equal proportions in a portfolio of securities $(j = 1, \ldots N)$ at day t and held until day m $(m = d + 1, d + 2, \ldots d + n)$. Unlike the cumulative average residuals the A.P.I. does not rebalance the portfolio for each day or period so as to obtain equal dollar investments at the start of that period. The A.P.I. is the more intuitively appealing measure and hence it has received a far wider usage than the cumulative average residuals. The differences between the results given by CU_T and the A.P.I. have often been small in the research studies done to date, but this was only because of the smallness of the residuals U_t – if the residuals U_t are fairly large or are measured over a longish period, then the differences between CU_T and the A.P.I. may be quite significant. Some studies have measured the CU_T or the A.P.I. over longish periods and here there may be some question marks over the results. This is because the beta values used in calculating the residuals may change significantly over time especially if the CU_T or the A.P.I. is consistently positive or consistently negative (see p. 98 for discussion of empirical research that has been done on the stability of betas for individual securities). Additionally, many influences affect a security's price over time and thus to say, for example, that any abnormal behaviour in the A.P.I. measured over a period of one year has been caused by just one event, say an earnings' announcement, will be tenuous to say the least.

The cumulative impact of the residuals is useful as it can show, for example the following:

(1) whether there has been any anticipation of the economic event prior to it being announced (i.e. an 'abnormal' build up in prices prior to the event). If the CU_T or A.P.I. is not averaging at zero, it signifies there is some special influence affecting the price (for example information leakage or anticipation).

(2) the time it takes for prices to settle down to their market model relationship after the economic event. In an efficient market we would expect the prices to settle down almost immediately with all the price reaction occurring on the first trading day after the event (this assumes that the 'event' has not caused the firm's systematic risk, B_j, to change).

Major studies on the impact of capitalisation issues (called 'stock splits' and 'stock dividends' in the United States) have been conducted in the United States by Fama, Fisher, Jensen and Roll[40] and Johnson,[41] in Canada by Finn,[42] and in the United Kingdom by Firth.[43] Unfortunately for research purposes capitalisation issues are normally announced at the same time as earnings and dividends and thus it becomes difficult to isolate the impact of the capitalisation issues. Johnson, Finn and Firth all used regression analysis (with the capitalisation issue as a dummy variable) to isolate the impact. Using this approach Finn and Firth found that capitalisation issues had no influence on share prices although Johnson implied otherwise.

All of these studies, however, showed that no profitable trading rules could be based on the announcement of a capitalisation issue, and thus that the market adjusted share prices instantaneously and accurately for the new information. Similar tests have been applied to securities when they go ex-dividend and these have also shown the market to be efficient. Both Pettit[44] and Watts[45] have investigated the market's reaction to dividend announcements. Although they reached different conclusions regarding the importance of dividend changes, they both found that all the price adjustment was over immediately after the announcement and thus the market had acted quickly in evaluating the information.

Research into the impact of other items of information on share prices in the United States includes the announcement of the following: large blocks of shares being bought and sold,[46] secondary market issues,[47] discount-rate changes,[48] earnings' announcements,[49] quarterly earnings' announcements,[50] accounting procedure changes[51] and earnings' estimates made by company officials.[52] These studies, which made heavy use of the residuals analysis approach, all showed the market to be relatively efficient – a few found some discrepancies but these were so small that their authors concluded that they provided no violation of the semi-strong form of market efficiency. (However, Jones and Litzenberger found that by using a mechanical strategy on quarterly earnings announcements, they could outperform the market average.[53] Jones extended his earlier study with Litzenberger by utilising filter rules to give buy signals and he again found that above-average returns could be gained.[54] These studies imply that the stock market does not adjust share prices precisely for all items of information (i.e. quarterly announcements).) It should be noted that most of the above tests were of announcements whose impact could not be measured precisely (see (2) on p. 129) and thus all that can be done is to see if prices reacted in the right direction; any conclusions about the correctness of the amount of the change is subjective.

Tests of the semi-strong form E.M.T. in the United Kingdom have been made by Firth. Using the residuals analysis approach he has examined the impact of the following.

(a) *Large investment holdings being built up in a firm.*[55] Figures 7.5 and 7.6 show the results of the study in pictorial form. The residuals, U_t, of the firms involved relative to the announcement day (day 0) are shown in Figure 7.5. Figure 7.6 shows the cumulative impact. Although there is no precise yardstick of what should happen when an announcement of the large holding has been made, we do expect it to increase the price (i.e. the takeover potential has increased). Figure 7.6 shows that the share prices rose significantly prior to the announcement. This may imply information leakage and/or strong pre-announcement buying by the investors building up their stakes (both influences are likely to have been present). Upon the announcement a large price rise occurred although a price decline followed thereafter. After ten days the residuals settled down to their normal relationship to the market index. Whilst the build up of prices prior to the announcement is not very satisfactory (implying some

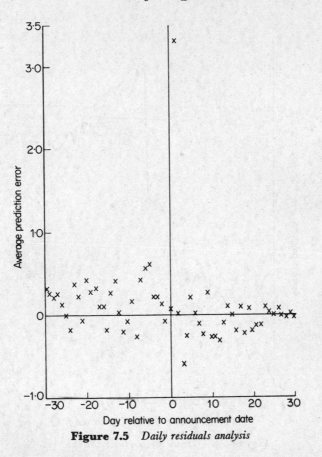

Figure 7.5   *Daily residuals analysis*

sort of dealing on knowledge that the market in general has not got), the price behaviour after the announcement seems fairly rational and 'efficient'.

(*b*) *Takeovers.*[56] The results showed that there was a build up in share prices in the bid-for companies in the thirty-day period prior to the bid. This was hypothesised to be the result of heavy pre-announcement buying by the bidding firm. Once the announcement of the takeover had been made, the stock market reacted both 'correctly' (there was no precise yardstick however) and quickly. This gave some support to the semi-strong form of market efficiency.

(*c*) *Earnings announcements of similar-type companies.*[57] This examined the influence that the earnings announcement of a firm had on

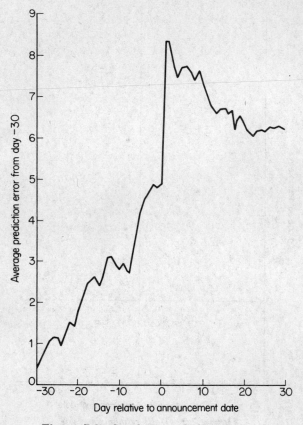

Figure 7.6 *Cumulative residuals analysis*

the share price of similar-type companies. Firth found that the reaction was in the direction expected although it was impossible to say whether the magnitude was correct. The findings showed that the stock market used relevant information in establishing share prices – this supports the efficient-market hypothesis.

(*d*) *Capitalisation issues.*[58] The findings showed that capitalisation issues had no impact on share prices and that the market acted rationally.

Fitzgerald has also examined the semi-strong version of the E.M.T. using U.K. data.[59] He found some evidence that portfolios constructed by buying shares recommended by certain advisers (stockbrokers, newspapers and investment advisory services) lead to significantly different returns (both abnormally good and abnormally bad) than those earned on the market index. Fitzgerald concluded by saying that the results suggested that the U.K. stock market is less efficient, in the semi-strong form, than the U.S. stock markets although he added that additional research was needed in this area.

Tests of the Strong-Form Efficient-Markets Theory

These tests are designed to appraise whether many investors have been able to obtain and profitably use inside information and whether any investors appear to have consistently superior success in the stock market. The former implies inefficiency and may well erode the average investor's confidence in investing if the amounts involved are very large. The latter implies that investment funds ought to be channelled to these successful investors so that the stock market's influence on resource allocation can be improved.

Some research has been done into whether investors who have access to inside information could have made profitable use of this. Both intuition and the research results have shown this to be so. For example, Niederhoffer and Osborne found that knowledge of unexecuted orders (orders placed by clients for buying and/or selling securities at specified prices which have not been executed at that point in time) could be used to derive profitable investment rules in the United States;[60] brokers have this information on unexecuted orders. Lorie and Niederhoffer studied 'insider trades' (that is the investment decisions of people who had inside information on the company concerned, for example directors) reported in the S.E.C.'s official summary of stock reports and found these were profitable in terms of outperforming the market average.[61] Additionally, knowledge of the insider's dealings provides profitable opportunities for other investors. Pratt and De Vere replicated Lorie and Niederhoffer's study on a larger sample and reached similar conclusions.[62] Jaffe also found that insider trading information contained in the Official Summary of Stock Reports could be used for profitable investment decisions.[63] He concluded that his results were inconsistent with the E.M.T. Collins derived a test to see whether investors who had information on historical segment earnings (that is where a firm's profits are given on a product line basis), data which were not publicly available at that time (pre-1970), could use this information to earn above-average returns.[64] He found that substantial profits could be made using these data.

Although there have only been a few empirical tests on the profitability of having and using inside information, the results show, as expected, that substantial returns can be made.

Very little work has been done on how extensive the use of inside information is and on the magnitude of the amounts involved. If these became very large the ordinary investors would become dissatisfied with the situation and substantial monies would be withdrawn from the stock market. More research on insider dealing is required even though it may be difficult to implement. This will help point out areas where the stock market can tighten up its 'regulatory' control.

There have been many research studies into the performance of investment portfolios although these have virtually all related to those with published results, for example investment trusts and unit trusts (called 'closed-end' and 'open-end' mutual funds in the United States). In addition there have also been some studies into the performance of individual investment analysts and investment advisory services. These studies are appropriate in examining the strong-form efficient-markets theory; any substantial and significant success for a portfolio implies that its manager either has special access to information or has exceptional skill.

There have been many studies into the performance of American mutual funds and these have used fairly sophisticated evaluation models. For example, the capital asset pricing model (see Chapter 5) has been used quite extensively; this allows the performance of the portfolio, for its level of risk, to be evaluated. All the major studies have found that mutual funds did no better than randomly constructed portfolios of similar risk – indeed many mutual funds showed a poorer performance thus indicating that their active investment management had done nothing to improve performance but had only added to the cost.*[65] These various studies have not been able to identify any consistently successful mutual funds.

* Many of the researchers have therefore concluded that investment managers should adopt a buy-and-hold policy. This raises an interesting point that has not been considered as yet: if everyone adopts a buy-and-hold policy there will be very little trading and this may affect market efficiency.

Firth conducted a study into the performance of unit trusts in the United Kingdom in the period 1965–75.[66] Using the capital asset pricing model Firth found that unit trusts did not outperform the market index for their given levels of risk. Many unit trusts had a significantly inferior performance in fact, and the results over all were probably poorer than those in the United States.

A smaller body of research has been conducted into the performance of individual investment recommendations. Such studies as there are suggest that few analysts or firms of advisers can claim above-average success with their forecasts.[67] Unfortunately there has been no research into the performance of private portfolios, and of course it can be argued that if any individual has exceptional skill in outperforming the market, then he will be operating solely on his own account. This problem is similar to that of examining investment rules; any strongly profitable strategy is unlikely to be revealed by its designers. The testing of the strong-form version of market efficiency therefore has to make do with analyses of published data.

The research on the strong-form E.M.T. has shown the following.

(*a*) Insider information can be used to earn above-average returns. This is intuitively obvious.

(*b*) Portfolios which publish their results have not been able to earn superior returns for their risk levels. This implies that the fund managers have neither access to insider information nor superior investment selection-timing abilities.

With regard to the above it must be emphasised that there has been no research into the extent of insider trading and thus its impact is not known (presumably, however, its impact has not been sufficient to make the average investor leave the market). Also there has been no research into the performance of private portfolios; any investors who have access to inside information or who have superior investment abilities are likely to be working for their own account and thus their performance is not available for inspection by researchers.

The Distribution of Security Returns

A good deal of attention has been paid by academic researchers to the distribution of security returns. This has been done for two major reasons, namely (1) if the distributions were found to be stationary, then probability statements about future returns could be made, and (2) if the distributions are not normally distributed, then the use of standard statistical tools, such as the serial-correlation analyses applied in testing for dependency, becomes invalid.

The evidence on the stationarity of distributions can be summarised thus:

(i) Share price distributions are not stationary over time. In the long term they tend to rise.

(ii) Distributions of share price changes (i.e. $P_t - P_{t-1}$) are not stationary over time. As share prices rise over time so does the value of share price changes.

(iii) Distributions of rates of return (both including and excluding dividends*) have been found to be relatively stable over time for the large majority of securities. The main advantages to investment analysts and portfolio managers of this stationarity is that probability statements of future rates of return can be made and, second, that past rates of return and their variability can be used to provide reasonable estimates of a share's future return and variability. The latter is of course very important in making portfolio theory viable in practice.

The second major reason for examining the distribution of price changes is to ascertain the validity of using standard statistical tools. The main area of research has centred on whether price changes and rates of return have a finite variance – if not, then this, strictly speaking, negates the use of standard deviations and variances in the analyses of dependence.

The early researchers in the field assumed that there was a finite variance and proceeded to test for independence with serial-correlation techniques. Some noticed that their data contained a higher than expected number of observations with high tails (large recordings); they did not proceed to investigate this further.[68] During the mid-1960s, however, Mandelbrot[69] and Fama[70] began to investigate the distributions of price changes more carefully. They found substantial evidence of high tail distributions[71] and these were classified as non-normal stable paretian distributions. The main characteristic of these for investment is that they have no finite variance and thus that the standard statistical analyses

---

* That is $(P_t - P_{t-1})/P_{t-1}$ without dividends or $[(P_t - P_{t-1}) + D_t]/P_{t-1}$ with dividends.

are inappropriate in measuring dependence. This in turn implies that many of the tests of linear dependence are spurious.

A number of methods to get around the infinite variance constraint have been proposed. One is the use of the mean absolute deviation as a measure of variability. Another, proposed by Fried,[72] is to divide the variations in returns into two parts with standard tests being applied for the body of the distribution and the tails being an 'unexplained variance'. There has been no real solution to the problem; most recent research has still used the standard statistical tools and a good deal of statistical work seems necessary before any more relevant tools can be developed. The main approach therefore appears to be that whilst the distributions of share price changes are not normal they are near enough so for the standard statistical tools to be applied.

Summary

This chapter has reviewed some of the major empirical tests of the efficient-markets theory. Most of the researchers involved in these studies have concluded that their investigations provided no significant evidence against the E.M.T. As described in Chapter 6, however, there do not appear to be any present-day tests which can provide sufficient evidence on the validity of the E.M.T. (using the generally accepted definition of market efficiency[73]); the evidence does support the competitive market hypothesis.

CHAPTER 8

Accounting and Efficient Markets

The efficient-markets theory says that share prices always fully reflect publicly available information and that any new items of information are instantaneously reflected in those prices. Thus any 'new' information of 'economic' value contained in annual or interim accounts should cause an immediate reaction in share prices as they adjust to reflect this information. 'New' information and 'economic' value are stressed as many data contained in accounting reports have already been reflected in share prices (i.e. anticipated by investors) and some data have no impact or no obvious impact on the economic value of the firm (for example directors' shareholdings). If one assumes that the market is efficient or 'reasonably' efficient, then this has certain implications for accounting.

First, the value of any item of accounting information, in terms of providing new economic information, can be ascertained. This is done by measuring the impact of an item on share prices. If the impact is significant, then this implies that information of real economic value is being imparted to the stock market. Having found that an accounting item does provide significant information the accountant and financial analyst should then seek to increase the benefits derived from this item (for example provide more detailed information on this item) or decrease the cost of providing the accounting information.

Second, the efficient-markets theory provides a yardstick by which various accounting alternatives can be evaluated. Thus if there are two ways of recording an item (for example the recording of potential capital gains tax on unrealised gains and the non-recording of the item), then the one which has the greatest impact on share prices is said, by the protagonists of the efficient-markets/

accounting school of thought, to be the method to use. A growing number of academics and practitioners are of this school, that is they believe in the predictive-ability criterion of the usefulness of accounting information – if a piece of accounting information has no impact on share prices, then it is of no value to investors and is therefore redundant. The efficient-markets theory has therefore provided a measurement yardstick which researchers can and have used to evaluate accounting disclosure levels and evaluate alternatives in accounting treatments.

A possible third but little considered implication is that the levels of accounting disclosure and the accounting methods to be used should be those that minimise the longer-term variability of share prices. The argument here is that by minimising the variability of share prices, the nearer the share price must be to the average 'intrinsic value'. In addition the cost of capital (the cost of financing the firm) will possibly be less for those firms with more stable share prices.

This chapter proceeds by briefly reviewing empirical studies that have been made into the following:

(*a*) the usefulness of accounting information for investors; and

(*b*) evaluating the impact of various accounting alternatives (i.e. alternative ways of accounting for an event) on share prices.

These studies have used an efficient-markets analysis framework and thus regard the predictive-ability criterion as of major importance in determining accounting practice. The chapter concludes by commenting upon the use of the predictive-ability criterion in evaluating accounting information and accounting alternatives.

Are Accounting Reports Useful to Investors?

Financial accounting reports (including the preliminary announcements of earnings which are usually made some time in advance of the release of the annual report) contain information of obvious economic value (earnings, assets, and so on) but much of this can be obtained or estimated from alternative sources (see Chapter 3, which briefly described the forecasting of corporate profits by investment analysts). In an efficient market (including the 'competitive-market' form) such sources will be utilised in setting share prices. The usefulness of accounting reports to investors is therefore represented by the additional information contained therein – i.e.

additional to the information already impounded in the market price. This suggests an obvious research methodology in appraising the usefulness of accounting reports. This methodology sets out to measure the impact on share prices of the release of accounting information and reports. It is therefore of a similar design to the semi-strong-form tests of market efficiency (described in Chapter 7). The assumptions and interpretation differ somewhat from the normal semi-strong market-efficiency tests. In the accounting research it is assumed that the market *is* efficient, i.e. 'correctly' impounding all publicly available information. On the release of the accounting information or report the share price of a firm may move to a new level, thus 'correctly' incorporating the 'new and additional' information contained in the report. The change in price in the immediate period covered by the announcement of the accounting data represents the economic value of that information. Note that unlike the other semi-strong-form tests it is not necessary to form *a priori* expectations of the impact of the accounting data (although as will be seen in the Ball and Brown study referred to below, some *a priori* expectations can be incorporated into the analyses).

Accounting reports are also useful in confirming prior expectations of market estimates of earnings. Thus reports give both new additional information (the impact of which can be captured in the above methodology) and confirm prior but uncertain earnings estimates derived by investors. This confirmation value of accounting reports is important but unfortunately there is no way of measuring its impact. Therefore most researchers have used only the evidence on the 'additional new information' provided by accounting reports in reaching conclusions as to the usefulness of such reports.

The first major study using the above research methodology was that by Ball and Brown.[1] Their first step was to estimate whether a firm had shown exceptionally good earnings (above those expected) or exceptionally poor earnings (below those expected). The expected earnings were derived from a model similar to the market model (see p. 93) but where the firm's income and the income of all firms are substituted for a firm's share price return and the return on the market. It is therefore of the following form:

$$\Delta I_{j,t-r} = \hat{a}_{1jt} + \hat{a}_{2jt}\,\Delta M_{j,t-r} + \hat{U}_{j,t-r},$$

where $\Delta I_{j,t-r}$ = the actual change in firm j's income, $\Delta M_{j,t-r}$ = the change in the average income of all firms, $\hat{a}_{1jt}$ and $\hat{a}_{2jt}$ are regression coefficients (a_2 is often known as a security's 'accounting beta'), $\hat{U}_{j,t-r}$ = a residual, $r = 1,2,3, \ldots t - 1$ = period.

From this model we can derive an expected change in earnings for firm j in period t by substituting in the value of ΔM_{jt}. The actual change in earnings of firm j are then compared with the expected earnings thus:

$$\hat{U}_{jt} = \Delta I_{jt} - \Delta \hat{I}_{jt},$$

where ΔI_{jt} = actual change, and $\Delta \hat{I}_{jt}$ = expected change.

If $\hat{U}_{jt}$ is positive, then this implies unexpectedly good earnings (termed 'good news' by Ball and Brown); if $\hat{U}_{jt}$ is negative this implies unexpectedly poor earnings (termed 'bad news').

Ball and Brown then measured the share price behaviour (The Abnormal Performance Index) of the shares of their sample firms using the market model approach. The results are shown pictorially in Figure 8.1. The upper panel shows that firms whose results were better than expected earned significantly above-average market returns (as given by the market model) in the period from one year prior to the release of the accounting information up to that date. Firms whose earnings were below those expected earned significantly below-average market returns thus providing a 'mirror image' with the top panel of Figure 8.1. From these results the following conclusions were reached.

(1) That the market is able to forecast earnings quite well. For example, most of the abnormal rise or fall in share prices took place before the earnings announcement showing relatively successful forecasting by investors.

(2) That about 50 per cent or more of the information about an individual firm that becomes available during a year is captured in that year's earnings figure.

(3) That on average only 10 to 15 per cent of the total price adjustment (over the entire period) took place in the month of announcement (month 0), i.e. the stock market had already adjusted share prices by around 85 to 90 per cent of its total adjustment, prior to the announcement.

(4) If an investor had been able to successfully predict which firms would experience above-expected earnings, at a date one year prior

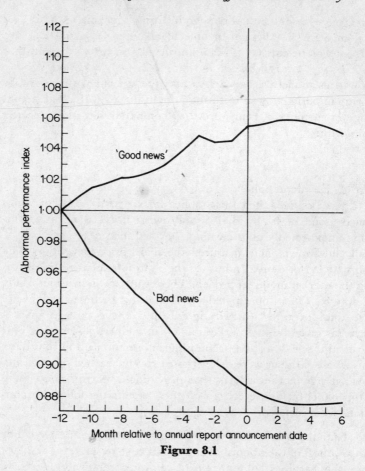

Figure 8.1

to the earnings announcement, they could have earned security returns of over 7 per cent above those expected from the market model. The returns earned from shares of firms who reported below-expected earnings were 10 per cent lower than those expected from the market model. Being able to predict the direction of earnings changes over a period of a year would therefore have resulted in large share price profits for an investor.

A similar study has been performed on Australian data by Brown.[2] He found similar results although the annual earnings figures imparted a relatively greater amount of new information; Brown found that 20–25 per cent of the total adjustment occurred on the announcement of the earnings figure, this comparing with 10–15 per cent for Ball and Brown's study. This indicated that earnings may be more difficult to forecast in Australia – the amount of information available to investors is certainly less than in the United States (for example, most Australian stocks only give half-yearly reports whereas in the United States most firms give quarterly results) and the resources devoted to formal investment analysis are also less.

Another early major study was that by Beaver.[3] He assessed the significance of accounting information by examining the impact of earnings announcements both on security returns and on the number of shares being traded in the stock market. (Unlike Ball and Brown he formed no prior estimates of the earnings that the market was expecting.)

Beaver's data consisted of 143 firms who made a total of 506 earnings announcements in the period 1961 through to 1965. He then measured the volume of trading for each week in the period eight weeks prior to the earnings' announcement to eight weeks after. The volume results are shown in Figure 8.2. Clearly there was a strong jump in investment activity in the week of the earnings announcement (week 0), with the average volume being 33 per

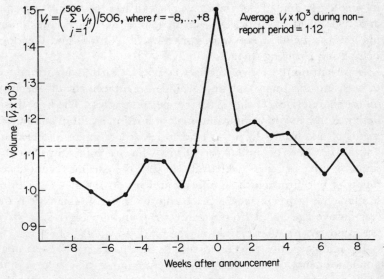

$$V_t = \left(\sum_{j=1}^{506} V_{jt} \right) / 506, \text{ where } t = -8, \ldots, +8$$

Average $V_t \times 10^3$ during non-report period = 1·12

Volume ($\bar{V}_t \times 10^3$)

Weeks after announcement

Figure 8.2

cent larger than the average volume in the other weeks. Subsequent to week 0 investment activity returned to more normal levels. Similar results were found for security price changes – the rate of change was far greater in week 0 than in other weeks.

These results showed that the announcement of earnings figures do have a significant impact on investment decision-taking. Additionally, the results indicated that the information value of the earnings announcement (changes in portfolio composition and in share price levels) took place immediately after the announcement.

Lev and Yahalomi replicated Beaver's methodology on Israeli data and surprisingly found that there was no noticeable investor reaction to earnings announcements.[4] They suggested that the long delay in publishing corporate results (on average six months after the year end) and capital-market inefficiencies were responsible for the findings.

Other researchers have also found that earnings announcements contain information which investors respond to immediately. Brown and Kennelly extended the Ball and Brown methodology to quarterly reports and found that the earnings announcements conveyed new and useful information for investors.[5] May[6] and Kiger,[7] using similar methodologies to Ball and Brown and Beaver, also found that quarterly earnings contained information which was helpful in predicting annual data and which lead to investment decisions and revision of share prices. Martin found that accounting information was useful in explaining price–earnings ratios and therefore helpful in predicting them.[8]

A variant on the above studies was that by Firth, who attempted to measure the impact of an earnings announcement of one firm on the share prices of other similar-type companies.[9] The hypothesis here was that any new information contained in earnings announcements of one firm is likely to lead to revised estimates of earnings and share prices of similar-type firms who are competitors in the same industry or market. Firth found that the earnings' announcements of one firm had a significant impact on the share prices of similar-type firms (the share price adjustment of similar-type firms was on average about 54 per cent of the announcing firm's share price movement, after extracting the market-wide factor).

In summary the research studies have shown that earnings announcements contain a significant amount of new information and the impact of this on share prices is completed very quickly.

The whole process of earnings announcements – interim accounts, accounts of similar-type firms and annual accounts – gives information which is utilised by investors.

Virtually all the research studies have concentrated on the earnings announcements, there being few studies on the impact of the release of the full set of accounts. Thus whilst the research has shown that earnings announcements contain valuable information, there have been no studies on whether other accounting data (sales, costs, balance-sheet items, and so on) give a great deal of new information. It will be difficult if not impossible to devise a workable research methodology which can successfully determine the informational impact of individual accounting items contained in annual accounts (presumably we would have to issue a report containing only one piece of information to assess its impact on share prices). However, research can and does need to be made into the impact of the release of the full set of accounts on investment decisions. It might be found, for example, that it is only the earnings figure which influences share prices and that the substantial amount of information given in the full set of accounts are not used by investors – the efficient-market theory would say that this information is therefore redundant.

A number of researchers have investigated the impact of changes in accounting procedures on share prices. Many of these changes contained no 'economically valuable' information (i.e. a change from straight-line depreciation to accelerated depreciation). In such cases there should be no significant impact on share prices if the stock market is efficient. The researchers have set out to investigate whether the market is efficient in respect of 'no economic value' and 'economic value' accounting procedure changes.

Some of the early researchers attempted to measure the impact of varying accounting procedures on the opinions of investment analysts. Dyckman,[10] for example, sent two identical (except for inventory valuation methods – one using FIFO the other LIFO) financial statements to financial analysts. He found that two of the three samples of analysts gave different share values depending on whether LIFO or FIFO was used. Jensen also found that financial analysts gave different earnings per share figures for firms depending upon the depreciation policy and inventory valuation method used.[11] These studies offered evidence that financial analysts did not 'see through' accounting procedures and that they gave different earnings per share estimates for varying ways of reporting identical information.

Bruns conducted a study to see if businessmen were influenced by varying accounting procedures relating to pricing, advertising and production decisions.[12] He found that the businessmen were able to 'see through' accounting procedures and so these did not influence their decisions. Barrett also found that the varying ways of consolidating accounts did not influence the opinions of financial analysts as long as sufficient information was given in the footnotes to the accounts.[13] Bruns's and Barrett's studies therefore indicated that businessmen and financial analysts were sophisticated enough to 'see through' accounting procedures. Other studies evaluating the impact of varying accounting procedures have used a simulation approach but these have also reached similar, rather conflicting findings.[14]

The above studies evaluated the impact of accounting procedures on estimates of earnings per share. However, an equally large body of research has looked at the impact of accounting changes on share prices. O'Donnell investigated whether different methods of accounting for depreciation and taxation had any impact on a firm's price–earnings ratio.[15] He found that investors were sophisticated enough to see through changes in accounting procedures: 'It follows that raising earnings by altering accounting procedures will not necessarily result, even in the short run, in higher stock prices.' Later, O'Donnell repeated his study on a larger sample and reached identical conclusions as above.[16] Similar studies by Summers,[17] Mlynarczyk,[18] Comiskey[19] and Gonedes[20] also found that investors were generally able to see through changes in accounting procedures – this of course supporting the efficient-markets theory (i.e. investors not being 'taken in' by accounting techniques which report different profit figures for the same economic event).

The above studies employed dividend or earnings' capitalisation models of share prices and thus no account of risk was taken. However, later studies, such as those referenced below, took explicit account of general market movements in share prices, by using the market model, and thus represent a much more sophisticated research methodology.

Archibald assessed the impact on share prices of the change over by companies to straight-line depreciation from accelerated depreciation.[21] The switch-over from accelerated depreciation to straight-line depreciation increases reported earnings per share and this could lead to an increase in share prices. The efficient-markets theory, however, says that investors recognise that the changes in depreciation methods do not represent an economic event and thus that there would be no change in share prices. Archibald found that the change in depreciation methods had no abnormal effect on share prices and thus his study supported the efficient-markets theory.

A similar study was conducted by Kaplan and Roll;[22] they looked at the impact of changes in accounting for investment tax credit and depreciation (straight-line and accelerated methods) on share prices. Their results generally supported the efficient-markets theory in that little abnormal movement in share prices was experienced for accounting changes of no economic consequence. (Kaplan and Roll did find some evidence of share prices reacting to changes in accounting treatments of investment credit. However, these results were probably due to certain statistical problems.)[23]

Ball conducted a study into the impact of differences in accounting treatments relating to a number of items such as inventory valuation, depreciation methods and accounting for subsidiaries.[24] Using a cross-sectional as opposed to a time-series model, Ball found that accounting changes had no impact on share prices.

Sunder examined the impact of inventory valuation methods on share prices.[25] He found that firms switching to LIFO (last-in-first-out) experienced an increase in share price in the months leading up to the change. Sunder expected some increase in share price, as in times of rising prices LIFO valuation methods decrease taxes, and these of course represent a real economic event. Subsequent to the accounting change there was no evidence of abnormal returns accruing to the sample firms. The share price rise prior to the accounting change indicated some anticipation by the market or information leakage. A number of researchers have also looked at the impact of inflation-adjusted accounting information on share prices. In the United Kingdom Morris investigated whether widely publicised estimates of inflation-adjusted earnings for 136 companies (other samples were also used) had any impact on share prices using the residual analysis technique.[26] He found there to be little impact, and from this he concluded that the market had already discounted the effect of inflation. (Although the stock market had not previously known of the inflation-adjusted earnings, they had, according to

Morris, incorporated the effects of inflation on firms when setting share prices. This is a somewhat shaky assumption, however. The inflation-adjusted estimates were produced by a large firm of stockbrokers and they may well have given these figures to client investors before making them publicly available (on which the research was based).) Morris also suggested that the inflation-adjusted earnings which were released did not have much predictive value. This is a rather strong claim to make as the inflation-adjusted earnings were generally far different from the historic cost figures. Although inflation-adjusted earnings may be no easier to predict, they surely impart some better knowledge of a firm's economic standing (which Morris claimed had already been discounted by the stock market). There is an alternative reason for their being no impact on share prices – that of the market being inefficient. Morris seemed to ignore this possibility altogether presumably because he started from an *a priori* position of regarding the market as efficient. Researchers in the United States have looked at the predictive value of inflation-adjusted accounting information. The results of the various studies have found the predictive value to be no better than that of conventional historical cost accounting.[27]

The above studies and others in the same area have sometimes reached inconclusive findings. Usually a small amount of share price reaction to non-important accounting information has been found and subjective estimates of how much this affects the E.M.T. have been made. This has, needless to say, resulted in varying interpretations and conclusions being reached. Studies which examined the impact of economically important accounting information have found that share prices moved in the direction expected. Whether the adjustment was sufficient, however, is impossible to measure and this has also led to differing conclusions as to the usefulness of accounting information.

The Predictive-Ability Criterion of Evaluating Accounting Information

The predictive-ability criterion of judging and determining accounting practices has received a large measure of support in recent years.[28] This criterion says that the decision as to whether to include a particular item in published accounts or whether to adopt a particular accounting treatment rests upon that item's or treatment's predictive ability, i.e. whether it enables investors to make more accurate forecasts of the future. For example, quarterly earnings announcements have been found to have some predictive power in forecasting full-year earnings and this has been recognised by investors who adjust share prices (see Chapter 4 and p. 72 in this chapter).* Most researchers' methodologies have involved investigating whether share prices have moved upon the release of a piece of accounting information – if they have, then it is said to be indicative of that information having predictive value, if not, then it is said to be indicative of the information having no predictive value. (Other researchers have evaluated the predictive-ability criterion by attempting to forecast accounting data into the future using some mechanical means. This is a more difficult yardstick to pass as it does not consider whether an investor can use the accounting data to predict future events.) However, there are a number of caveats to the use of the predictive-ability criterion. First, of course, there is the assumption that the market is efficient. If this is not so, then the fact that there is little or no movement in share prices upon the release of certain accounting information does not prove that the accounting information is of no value – it may be that the market is incapable of interpreting perfectly useful accounting information in share price values (see the comments on Morris's study, page 149). Chapter 6 concluded by saying that there is no strong proof supporting the E.M.T. and that the onus of proving efficiency rests perhaps more on the protagonists of market efficiency. Thus the 'efficient-market' assumption backing the predictive-ability criterion is somewhat weak. Some of the results from academic studies, however, have been so significant that measures of usefulness of published data or accounting treatments can be legitimately gleaned from share price behaviour.

Apart from the caveat of the efficient-markets assumption there is also the fact that accounting data, even though not providing new information, do confirm prior expectations. The confirmation value of accounting data is very important and probably leads to

---

* There appears to be no simple mechanical way in which annual earnings figures can be accurately extrapolated into the future (see p. 70). Investors do, however, adjust share prices on the announcement of annual earnings, thus showing, according to the E.M.T., that they are of predictive value. This apparent conflict can be resolved in that investors may use fairly sophisticated methods of prediction and incorporate additional information in their evaluations.

more stable stock market conditions (i.e. investors getting feedback on their forecasts). Unfortunately, as mentioned before, the efficient-markets studies have not been able to capture the 'confirmation' impact of accounting data.

Another major caveat is that accounting reports provide information to a far wider body of people than investors in the equity market. Thus the criterion of usefulness should be addressed to the usefulness to all the users of accounts (for example fixed-interest investors, employees, trade unions, consumers, government, society at large). There has in fact been a growing acceptance of the need to report to a wider number of 'interested' parties – that is, individuals and groups of individuals who have an interest in the performance and the business policies of the firm. Both the United States with the *Trueblood Report*[29] and the United Kingdom with the *Corporate Report*[30] have emphasised the need for more relevant disclosure for other than equity shareholder interested parties. Unfortunately the research methodologies discussed above relate solely to the information content given to equity investors. If only one set of accounts is to be published for all users, then the criterion should presumably be the set of accounts that maximises the usefulness to all users (some sort of trade-off will amost certainly have to be made). The efficiency of such reports cannot then of course be properly assessed by efficient-market studies. Occasionally there have been suggestions that a number of different accounts could be issued by a firm depending on who the recipient is. The efficient-markets predictive-ability criterion could then be used to assess the accounts that are sent to shareholders. It seems unlikely, however, that the multiple accounts will be produced – the cost involved and the probable confusion created (at least initially) outweigh possible advantages.

The most important use of accounting information is that supplied to management. Management relies heavily on accounting data in its role of decision-takers, and of course it is such decisions which have a vitally important bearing on corporate earnings, employment conditions and economic growth. Whilst investors do not receive management accounting information, the financial accounts they do get are usually prepared from the management accounting data (i.e. management deciding that a completely separate financial accounting system would involve too much duplication and, more importantly, too much expense). Thus the form of financial accounts is not specified solely by the predictive-ability criterion; it has to make do with any constraints imposed by the prevailing management accounting systems. (Management can of course operate a completely separate financial accounting system, free from any constraints imposed by the management accounting system, if the cost of doing so is outweighed by the benefits accruing to the users of financial accounts.) Thus to measure the usefulness of accounting data on the 'predictive ability for equity investors' criteria, is again a not entirely satisfactory procedure.

Summary

This chapter has discussed accounting information and its relationship with efficient markets. Specifically the predictive-ability criterion of accounting data has been introduced and a number of the major empirical studies relating thereto have been reviewed. The predictive-ability criterion rests upon the assumption that the stock market is efficient and thus that investors' reactions to accounting data represent the new additional economically valuable information contained therein. However, the major problem with using this criterion is that the empirical tests have dealt solely with the predictive ability for equity investors. No account has been taken of the informational content of accounting data for other users of accounts and it is these users who have been growing in importance in the last few years.

The empirical studies have shown that accounting information, and especially earnings' announcements, do have an impact on the stock market, both for the reporting company's securities and for other firm's securities. The market appears to respond very rapidly to accounting information and this of course is consistent with an efficient market. There appears to be no simple way of utilising accounting data to earn profits in excess of the market – it will take a fairly original model (either a very sophisticated one or a very 'unlikely' one) utilising accounting data to earn superior returns. Because accounting information is useful to investors, one obvious implication is that more frequent accounting information released quickly after the period to which it relates should be made (subject to cost considerations). Thus monthly sales, gross profits, cash balances, orders on hand, and so on, could be released (along with figures from prior periods) say within a couple of weeks after the month end. Although it is difficult to see this happening in the United Kingdom in the near future, it is an obvious conclusion to be drawn from the efficient-markets studies.

The evidence relating to the impact of changes in accounting procedures on share prices is more tenuous – many results have shown slight departures from those expected under efficient-market conditions. Whether this departure is sufficient to negate the E.M.T. remains a subjective point and has led to some differences of academic opinion. Most of the researchers involved have been prepared to conclude from their studies, however, that investors do 'see through' accounting procedures, and that the predictive-ability criterion is an adequate yardstick.

The chapter has shown that the findings relating to accounting and efficient markets is somewhat inconclusive, and clearly much more research is needed. This should be directed both at establishing adequate measurements of performance and in solving various statistical problems inherent in the research. Additionally, of course, basic research in the United Kingdom is needed and fortunately there are some indications that researchers are responding to this.

CHAPTER 9

Concluding Remarks

We started the book by describing the role of the stock market. In doing this we introduced the concept of an 'efficient market', that is one which provides 'accurate' share pricing such that resource allocation is optimised. An efficient market is obtained partially by having a highly competitive, well-regulated and expert stock exchange. Chapters 2 and 3 led on from this by describing the actual methods used by investment analysts in evaluating share prices. Clearly a high level of detailed analyses are being undertaken by investment analysts in their work. Chapter 4 reviewed some empirical studies that have been made into the forecasting of earnings and other accounting data by purely statistical means. These studies have found there to be little predictive ability in using statistical extrapolations of past data – hence the work of investment analysts is made that much more difficult; there are no mechanical ways of successfully forecasting future earnings data (except from interim accounts).

From the work carried out by investment analysts we then proceeded to discuss the capital asset pricing model (C.A.P.M.) which presents us with a theoretical structure for the setting of share prices. A number of empirical tests have been made into the applicability of the C.A.P.M. for actual share price data. These have broadly found that the C.A.P.M. fits portfolios of shares quite well but that the model provides a much poorer explanation of individual security returns. From these results it is clear that a lot more work is needed in this area both in specifying the basic model and in establishing the stability of parameters. The next chapter formally presented the efficient-markets model, discussed the difficulties in testing it, and described the institutional arrangements in the United Kingdom which help towards creating an efficient market. Chapter 7 reviewed the large body of research that has been conducted into the efficient-markets theory (E.M.T.). It was concluded that the research generally supported the E.M.T. although, as suggested in the prior chapter, there is no conclusive way of testing the theory. Finally, Chapter 8 looked at the implications of the E.M.T. for accountancy and accounting research. Thus the book has come full circle; we started off by introducing the concept of an efficient market, we then described the methods used by analysts to determine 'accurate' share prices and finally reviewed the evidence for and against the E.M.T. as a description of actual behaviour.

Implications

A number of conclusions can be drawn from the theories and studies reviewed in the book. These include implications for society at large, investors, investment analysts, accounting, and the institutional arrangements of the stock market as well as implications and suggestions for future research.

(1) *Society at large.* The major stock exchanges appear to offer competitive market-places and there is little evidence of individual investors being able to earn consistently superior returns. However, it seems doubtful if any stock market can claim to be fully 'efficient' in the sense of providing consistently accurate share values so as to help optimise resource allocation. Whether any outside regulation (for example Government regulation) of the capital market is required is a very pertinent question; there are certainly some points in favour of this. (However, the fact that millions of investors are prepared to invest directly or indirectly in the stock market is some evidence that the market is providing a reasonably 'useful' function).

(2) *Investors and investment analysts.* There do not appear to be any easy ways of earning consistently superior investment returns. Additionally, no strong evidence has come to light that individual investors have been able to earn superior returns. A major implication of the E.M.T. studies is that the benefits of investment analysis are free to all (i.e. impounded in current share prices) and thus an investor should not expend any resources on investment analysis himself. This is subject to the caveat that the investor or analyst is unable to produce superior investment analysis. Thus it may be

possible with a good deal of sophisticated research or a good deal of luck to derive an investment rule or a methodology which earns superior returns (it must be stressed, however, that the chances of finding such a rule or methodology are very small given the competitive nature of the market). If the rule or methodology can be kept secret, then superior returns may be earned.

(3) *Accounting.* The predictive-ability criterion of evaluating accounting information has used an efficient-markets framework in its research methodology. However, this framework does not provide an entirely satisfactory measurement yardstick. Thus a considerable amount of subjective and intuitive judgement skill has to be exercised in setting accounting standards (predictive ability is a valid concept but there appears to be no adequate quantitative method of measuring accounting data in this way).

(4) *Institutional arrangements.* There is evidence that certain types of information do influence share prices (for example earnings announcements) and thus greater amounts of this information, and more speedy announcements of it, will help improve market efficiency. Specific examples of these instances include more frequent and speedy earnings announcements and speeding up the announcement and the lowering of the disclosure level of large investment stakes having been built up (see p. 132). In addition, the stock market should strive to improve its regulatory control over insider trading, although it is acknowledged that it is impossible to eradicate it altogether.

(5) *Research.* More research is needed into specifying the form of the theoretical structure of the setting of share prices. This will enable the models used in the empirical tests of efficient markets and accounting to be better specified. Additionally, of course, greater amounts of research are needed in stock markets outside of the United States. The recently built data banks in the United Kingdom should enable some high-quality work to be done on the U.K. stock market.

Hopefully the book has highlighted major research studies, completed elsewhere, that could be usefully replicated and extended in the United Kingdom. In addition it is hoped that the book has enabled the reader to understand the recent developments in capital-market theory and to place them in context with practical investment analysis.

Notes and References

Chapter 1

1. See W. J. Baumol, *The Stock Market and Economic Efficiency* (Fordham University Press, 1965) for a discussion of the requirements of a well-run market place.

2. A. J. Merrett and A. Sykes, 'Return on Equities and Fixed Interest Securities 1919–1966' *District Bank Review* (June 1966).

3. L. Fisher and J. H. Lorie, 'Rates of Return on Investments in Common Stocks', *Journal of Business*, vol. 37 (January 1964), 'Rates of Return on Investments in Common Stock, The Year by Year Record, 1926–65', *Journal of Business*, vol. 41 (July 1968), 'Some Studies of Variability of Returns on Investment in Common Stocks', *Journal of Business*, vol. 43 (April 1970).

4. '. . . , The Year by Year Record'.

5. 'Some Studies of Variability of Returns on Investment'.

6. A. Cowles, *Common Stock Indexes, 1871–1937*, Cowles Commission Monograph (1938).

7. R. L. Weil, 'Realized Interest Rates and Bondholders' Returns', *American Economic Review*, vol. 60 (June 1970); and L. Fisher and R. L. Weil, 'Coping with the Risk of Interest Rate Fluctuations: Return to Bondholders from Naive and Optimal Strategies', *Journal of Business*, vol. 44 (October 1971).

8. For a detailed description of the jobbing system, see one of the standard texts on the mechanisms of the stock exchange, for example R. J. Briston, *The Stock Exchange and Investment Analysis*, 3rd edn. (London: Allen & Unwin, 1975) and E. V. Morgan and W. A. Thomas, *The Stock Exchange. Its History and Functions* (London: Elek, 1962).

9. This is not a detailed coverage of the techniques of investment

analysis; for a detailed discussion of this in the United Kingdom, see M. A. Firth, *Investment Analysis: Techniques of Appraising the British Stock Market* (London: Harper & Row, 1975).

Chapter 2

1. For an introduction to portfolio theory, see T. Ryan, *Portfolio Analysis* (London: Macmillan, forthcoming).

2. For a discussion of this aspect of growth stocks, see D. Durand, 'Growth Stocks and the Petersburg Paradox', *Journal of Finance*, vol. 12 (September 1957).

3. See J. F. Weston and E. F. Brigham, *Managerial Finance* (New York: Holt, Rinehart & Winston, 1975) for a discussion of certainty equivalents.

4. Both the dividend yield and the price–earnings ratio are capable of several definitions as there are different definitions of 'earnings per share' and of 'dividends'. For a description of the appropriate measurements and the problems involved, see Firth, *Investment Analysis*.

5. J. B. Cohen and E. D. Zinbarg, *Investment Analysis and Portfolio Management* (Homewood, Ill.: Irwin, 1967).

6. For an interesting discussion on this topic, see C. C. Holt, 'The Influence of Growth Duration on Share Prices', *Journal of Finance* (December 1962).

7. See M. A. Firth, *Forecasting Methods for Management* (London: Edward Arnold, 1977) for an introductory discussion of regression analysis.

8. V. S. Whitbeck and M. Kisor Jr, 'A New Tool in Investment Decision Making', *Financial Analysts Journal* (May–June 1963).

9. R. S. Bower and D. M. Bower, 'Risk and the Valuation of Common Stock', *Journal of Political Economy* (May–June 1969).

10. D. M. Ahlers, 'SEM: A Security Evaluation Model', in *Analytical Methods in Banking*, ed. K. J. Cohen and F. S. Hammer (Homewood, Ill.: Irwin, 1966).

11. D. Weaver and M. G. Hall, 'The Evaluation of Ordinary Shares Using a Computer', *Journal of the Institute of Actuaries* (September 1967).

12. M. J. Gordon, *The Investment, Financing and Valuation of the Corporation* (Homewood, Ill.: Irwin, 1962).

13. H. Benishay, 'Variability in Earnings–Price Ratios of Corporate Equities', *American Economic Review*, vol. 51 (1961).

14. E. M. Lerner and W. T. Carleton, 'The Integration of Capital Budgeting and Stock Valuation', *American Economic Review*, vol. 54 (September 1964), and *A Theory of Financial Analysis* (New York: Harcourt Brace, 1966).

15. M. Keenan, 'Models of Equity Valuation: The Great Serm Bubble', *Journal of Finance*, May, 1970. In this paper Keenan reported the results of testing the predictive ability of a number of models. The results he arrived at were disappointing and he concluded that a lot more research would have to be done into respecifying the models and in improving basic earnings forecasts before the approach could achieve successful results.

16. M. G. Hall, 'Forecasting Movements in the U.K. Equity Market', in *Mathematics in the Stock Exchange* (The Institute of Mathematics and its Applications, 1972).

17. The source for the figure is Firth, *Investment Analysis*.

Chapter 3

1. H. A. Latané and D. L. Tuttle, 'An Analysis of Common Stock Price Ratios', *Southern Economic Journal*, vol. 33 (January 1967).

2. M. Kisor and V. A. Messner, 'The Filter Approach and Earnings Forecasts – Part One', private manuscript (June 1968).

3. For a description of these items, see E. S. Hendriksen, *Accounting Theory* (Homewood, Ill.: Irwin, 1970).

4. For a discussion of income and capital valuation, see C. Sutcliffe, *Economics versus Accountancy* (London: Macmillan, forthcoming).

5. L. Spacek, 'Business Success Requires an Understanding of Unsolved Problems of Accounting and Financial Reporting', in *Modern Developments in Investment Management*, ed. J. Lorie and R. A. Brealey (New York: Praeger, 1972).

6. R. J. Chambers, 'Financial Information and the Securities Market', *Abacus*, vol. 1, no. 1 (September 1965).

7. R. Ball, 'Changes in Accounting Techniques and Stock Prices', Empirical Research in Accounting: Selected Studies 1972, *Journal of Accounting Research*, supplement (1972).

8. See Firth, *Forecasting Methods for Management*, for a description of forecasting techniques in use by management.

9. For a detailed description of company forecasting, including longer-term factors, see Firth, *Investment Analysis*.

10. These methods have been described in some detail in ibid. and M. A. Firth, 'Quantitative Approaches to Forecasting Corporate Profits', *Management Decision* (Winter 1975).

11. For examples of specific probabilistic and simulation model applications in forecasting, see P. G. Neild, W. T. Seward and A. R. Good, 'Company Models as an Aid to Evaluation: London Brick', *Investment Analyst*, no. 35 (June 1973); W. H. Wagner *et al.*, 'Telecommunications Earnings Estimation Model (TEEM): Evaluation', in *Corporate Simulation Models*, ed. A. N. Schrieber (Washington University Press, 1970); and J. A. Olsen and T. A. Blaney, 'Forecasting by Probabilities: The Copper Industry', *Financial Analysts Journal*, vol. 24 (March–April 1968).

12. This is taken from Firth, *Investment Analysis*.

13. Also taken from ibid.

14. See, for example, ibid. For summary articles on forecasting of corporate profits, see M. A. Firth, 'The Forecasting of Company Profits', *Accountants Review* (March 1975) and Firth, 'Quantitative Approaches to Forecasting Corporate Profits'.

Chapter 4

1. For a discussion of income smoothing and conditions where this is favourable, see N. Gonedes, 'Income Smoothing Behavior under Selected Stochastic Processes', *Journal of Business*, vol. 45 (October 1972).

2. See R. Ball, B. Lev and R. Watts, 'Income Changes and Balance Sheet Compositions', *Journal of Accounting Research*, vol. 11 (Autumn 1973).

3. I. M. D. Little, 'Higgledy Piggledy Growth', *Bulletin of the Oxford Institute of Statistics* (November 1962).

4. I. M. D. Little and A. C. Rayner, *Higgledy Piggledy Growth Again* (Oxford: Blackwell, 1966).

5. J. Lintner and R. R. Glauber, 'Higgledy Piggledy Growth in America', Paper for the Seminar on the Analysis of Security Prices (University of Chicago May 1967), reprinted in *Modern Developments in Investment Management* (New York: Praeger, 1972).

6. A firm which provides statistics relating to stock exchange quoted American corporations.

7. J. Lintner and R. R. Glauber, 'Further Observations on Higgledy Piggledy Growth', Paper for the Seminar on the Analysis of Security Prices (University of Chicago, May 1969).

8. J. E. Murphy, Jr, 'Relative Growth of Earnings per Share – Past and Future', *Financial Analysts Journal*, vol. 22 (November–December 1966).

9. R. A. Brealey, 'The Character of Earnings Changes', Paper for the Seminar on the Analysis of Security Prices (University of Chicago, May 1967).

10. R. H. Trent, 'Corporate Growth Rates: An Analysis of their Intertemporal Association', *Southern Journal of Business*, vol. 4 (October 1969).

11. R. Ball and R. Watts, 'Some Time Series Properties of Accounting Income', *Journal of Finance*, vol. 27 (June 1972).

12. W. Beaver, 'The Time Series Behavior of Earnings', Empirical Research in Accounting: Selected Studies 1970, *Journal of Accounting Research*, supplement (1970).

13. See W. Frank, 'A Study of the Predictive Significance of Two Income Measures', *Journal of Accounting Research* (1969); and J. K. Simmons and J. Gray, 'An Investigation of the Effect of Differing Accounting Frameworks on the Prediction of Net Income', *Accounting Review*, vol. 44 (October, 1969).

14. 'Higgledy Piggledy Growth in America'.

15. Y. Peles, 'Amortization of Advertising Expenditures in the Financial Statements', *Journal of Accounting Research*, vol. 8 (Spring 1970).

16. See R. Ball and P. Brown, 'Some Preliminary Findings on the Association between the Earnings of a Firm, Its Industry and the Economy', Empirical Research in Accounting: Selected Studies, 1967, *Journal of Accounting Research*, supplement (1967).

17. D. Green and J. Segall, 'The Predictive Power of First-Quarter Earnings Reports' *Journal of Business*, vol. 40 (January 1967).

18. D. Green and J. Segall, 'The Predictive Power of First-Quarter Earnings Reports: A Replication', Empirical Research in Accounting: Selected Studies, 1966, *Journal of Accounting Research*, supplement (1966).

19. P. Brown and V. Niederhoffer, 'The Predictive Content of Quarterly Earnings', *Journal of Business*, vol. 41 (October, 1968).

20. See D. Green and J. Segall, 'Brickbats and Straw Men: A Reply to Brown and Niederhoffer', *Journal of Business*, vol. 41 (October 1968); V. Niederhoffer, 'The Predictive Content of First Quarter Earnings Reports', *Journal of Business*, vol. 43 (January 1970); D. Green and J. Segall, 'Return of Strawman', *Journal of Business*, vol. 43 (January 1970); and, in the same issue, Holton and Welsch, 'Discussions of D. Green and J. Segall, "The Predictive Power of First-Quarter Earnings Reports: A Replication" ', for a discussion of Green and Segall's 1966 article and arguments about the interpretation of results.

21. R. Coates, 'The Predictive Content of Interim Reports – A Time Series Analysis', Empirical Research in Accounting: Selected Studies, 1972, *Journal of Accounting Research*, supplement, vol. 10 (1972).

22. P. Brown and J. W. Kennelly, 'The Informational Content of Quarterly Earnings: An Extension and Some Further Evidence', *Journal of Business*, vol. 45 (July 1972).

23. F. K. Reilly, D. L. Morgenson and M. West, 'The Predictive Ability of Alternative Parts of Interim Financial Statements', Empirical Research in Accounting: Selected Studies, 1972, *Journal of Accounting Research*, supplement, vol. 10 (1972).

24. H. A. Latané, D. L. Tuttle and C. P. Jones, 'E/P Ratios *v* Changes in Earnings in Forecasting Future Price Changes', *Financial Analysts Journal*, vol. 25 (January–February 1969).

25. C. P. Jones and R. H. Litzenberger, 'Quarterly Earnings Reports and Intermediate Stock Price Trends', *Journal of Finance*, vol. 25 (March 1970).

26. See M. A. Firth, 'The Impact of Earnings Announcements on the Share Price Behaviour of Similar Type Firms', *Economic Journal* (June 1976).

27. None of the research studies have found precise yardsticks which apply in every case. Indeed one would be surprised if such precision were found in any economic model.

28. E. I. Altman, 'Financial Ratios, Discriminant Analysis and the Prediction of Corporate Bankruptcy', *Journal of Finance*, vol. 23 (September 1968).

29. J. R. Ramser and L. O. Foster, 'A Demonstration of Ratio Analysis', *Bulletin No. 40*, Bureau of Business Research, University of Illinois (1931).

30. P. J. Fitzpatrick, 'A Comparison of Ratios of Successful

Industrial Enterprises with those of Failed Firms', *Certified Public Accountant*, vol. 12 (October, November and December 1932).

31. C. H. Winakor and R. F. Smith, 'Changes in Financial Structure of Unsuccessful Industrial Companies', *Bulletin No. 51*, Bureau of Economic Research, University of Illinois (1935).

32. C. L. Merwin, *Financing Small Corporations in Five Manufacturing Industries 1926–36* (New York: National Bureau of Economic Research, 1942).

33. R. J. Saulnier, H. G. Halcrow and N. H. Jacoby, *Federal Lending and Loan Insurance* (Princeton University Press, 1958).

34. G. H. Moore and T. R. Atkinson, 'Risks and Returns in Small Business Financing', in *Towards a Firmer Basis of Economic Policy*, 41st Annual Report, National Bureau of Economic Research (1961).

35. M. H. Seiden, 'Trade Credit: A Quantitative and Qualitative Analysis', in *Tested Knowledge of Business Cycles*, 42nd Annual Report, National Bureau of Economic Research (1962).

36. W. H. Beaver, 'Financial Ratios as Predictors of Failures', Empirical Research in Accounting: Selected Studies, 1966, *Journal of Accounting Research*, supplement, vol. 4 (1966).

37. For each 'failed' firm, a non-failed firm in the same industry and of the same size was paired against it. Generally the paired sample technique is designed to control for various factors which are believed to be unrelated to the item being studied (i.e. bankruptcy). However, both size and industry factors are related to the occurrence of bankruptcy and hence Beaver's methodology prevents their contribution to predicting corporate bankruptcy being measured.

38. W. H. Beaver, 'Market Prices, Financial Ratios, and the Prediction of Failure', *Journal of Accounting Research*, vol. 6 (Autumn 1968).

39. J. W. Wilcox, 'A Prediction of Business Failure Using Accounting Data', Empirical Research in Accounting: Selected Studies, 1973, *Journal of Accounting Research*, supplement, vol. II (1973).

40. E. I. Altman, 'Financial Ratios, Discriminant Analysis', and *Corporate Bankruptcy in America* (Lexington: Heath, 1971).

41. One of the earliest studies using M. D. A. in financial research was by J. E. Walter, 'A Discriminant Function for Earnings Price Ratios of Large Industrial Corporations', *Review of Economics and Statistics*, vol. 41 (February 1959). He used it in classifying high and

low price–earnings ratio firms. K. V. Smith conducted a similar study when he used M.D.A. to classify firms into standard investment categories – Classification of Investment Securities Using MDA', *Institute Paper No. 101*, Institute for Research in the Behavioral, Economic and Management Sciences, Purdue University (1965).

42. R. Taffler, 'Finding Those Firms in Danger', *Accountancy Age* (16 July 1976).

43. P. A. Meyer and H. W. Pifer, 'Prediction of Bank Failures, *Journal of Finance*, vol. 25 (September 1970).

44. For a comparison of the two methods, see G. Ladd, 'Linear Probability Functions and Discriminant Functions', *Econometrica*, vol. 33 (October 1965).

45. R. Westerfield, 'Pre-Bankruptcy Stock Price Performance', *Working Paper*, University of Pennsylvania (Autumn 1970).

46. Other studies into the prediction of corporate failures include R. O. Admister, 'An Empirical Test of Financial Ratio Analysis for Small Business Failure Prediction', *Journal of Financial and Quantitative Analysis*, vol. 7 (March 1972); E. I. Altman, 'Corporate Bankruptcy Potential, Stockholder Returns and Share Valuation', *Journal of Finance*, vol. 24 (December 1969), 'Railroad Bankruptcy Potential', *Journal of Finance*, vol. 26 (May 1971), and 'Predicting Railroad Bankruptcies in America', *Bell Journal of Economics and Management Science*, vol. 4 (Spring 1973); N. Baxter, 'Leverage, Risk and Ruin and Cost of Capital', *Journal of Finance*, vol. 22 (September 1967); M. Blum, 'The Failing Company Doctrine', Ph.D. dissertation, Columbia University (1969); and E. A. Deakin, 'A Discriminant Analysis of Predictors of Business Failure', *Journal of Accounting Research*, vol. 10 (Spring 1972).

47. Altman, for example, found that liquidity ratios were useful as a predictor yet Beaver found them to be very poor.

48. See K. Lewis, 'Business Failures – Another Example of the Analysis of Failure Data', *Journal of the American Statistical Association*, vol. 49 (December 1954); and H. N. Broom and J. G. Longenecker, *Small Business Management* (Cincinnati: South-Western Publishing Co., 1971).

49. L. Fisher, 'Determinants of Risk Premiums on Corporate Bonds', *Journal of Political Economy*, vol. 67 (June 1959).

50. See, for example, G. Harold, *Bond Ratings as an Investment Guide* (New York: Ronald Press, 1938); O. K. Burrell, *A Study*

in Investment Mortality, Bureau of Business Research, School of Business Administration, University of Oregon (1947); and W. B. Hickman, *Corporate Bond Quality and Investor Experience* (Princeton University Press for the National Bureau of Economic Research, 1958).

51. See A. C. Esokait, 'The Men Who Make Treasures Tremble', *Forbes* (1 September 1970).

52. J. O. Horrigan, 'The Determination of Long-Term Credit Standing with Financial Ratios', Empirical Research in Accounting: Selected Studies, 1966, *Journal of Accounting Research*, vol. 4, supplement (1966).

53. If a firm issues two or more loan stocks (bonds), then they are often ranked in preference as regards payment of interest and principal. Bonds which do not have first preference are described as 'subordinated' and they are more risky than the non-subordinated bonds of the firm.

54. R. R. West, 'An Alternative Approach to Predicting Corporate Bond Ratings', *Journal of Accounting Research*, vol. 8 (Spring 1970).

55. G. E. Pinches and K. A. Mingo, 'A Multivariate Analysis of Industrial Bond Ratings', *Journal of Finance*, vol. 28 (March 1973).

56. T. F. Pogue and R. M. Soldofsky, 'What's in a Bond Rating', *Journal of Financial and Quantitative Analysis*, vol. 4 (June 1969).

57. W. T. Carleton and E. M. Lerner, 'Statistical Credit Scoring of Municipal Bonds', *Journal of Money, Credit and Banking*, vol. 1 (November 1969).

58. J. J. Horton Jr, 'Statistical Classification of Municipal Bonds', *Journal of Bank Research*, vol. i (Autumn 1970).

59. See Y. E. Orgler, 'A Credit Scoring Model for Commercial Loans', *Journal of Money, Credit and Banking*, vol. 2 (November 1970).

60. D. D. Hester, 'An Empirical Examination of a Commercial Bank Loan Offer Function', *Yale Economic Essays*, vol. 2 (Spring 1962).

61. K. J. Cohen, C. Gilmore and F. A. Singer, 'Bank Procedures for Analyzing Business Loan Applications', in *Analytical Methods in Banking*, ed. K. J. Cohen and F. S. Hammer (Homewood, Ill.: Irwin, 1966).

62. A. W. Wojnilower, *The Quality of Bank Loans*, Occasional Paper 82, National Bureau of Economic Research (1962).

63. H. K. Wu, 'Bank Examiner Criticism, Bank Loan Defaults, and Bank Loan Quality', *Journal of Finance* (September 1969).

64. Orgler, 'A Credit Scoring Model for Commercial Loans'.

65. A. Singh, *Takeovers: Their Relevance to the Stock Market and the Theory of the Firm* (Cambridge University Press, 1971).

66. D. Kuehn, *Takeovers and the Theory of the Firm* (London: Macmillan, 1975).

67. J. Tzoannos and J. M. Samuels, 'Mergers and Takeovers: The Financial Characteristics of Companies Involved', *Journal of Business Finance* (Autumn 1972).

68. J. M. Samuels and J. Tzoannos, 'Takeovers and Share Price Evaluation', *Business Ratios* (Summer 1970).

69. G. D. Newbould, *Management and Merger Activity* (Liverpool: Guthstead, 1970).

70. A. Buckley, 'A Profile of Industrial Acquisitions in 1971', *Accounting and Business Research* (Autumn 1972).

71. M. A. Firth, 'A Multivariate Analysis of the Financial Characteristics of Acquired Firms', unpublished MS. (1976).

72. R. A. Taussig and S. L. Hayes, 'Cash Takeovers and Accounting Valuations', *Accounting Review* (January 1968).

73. D. L. Stevens, 'Financial Characteristics of Merged Firms: A Multivariate Analysis', *Journal of Financial and Quantitative Analysis* vol. 8 (March 1973).

74. R. J. Monroe and M. A. Simkowitz, 'Investment Characteristics of Conglomerate Targets: A Discriminant Analysis', *Southern Journal of Business* (November 1971).

Chapter 5

1. W. F. Sharpe, 'Capital Asset Prices: A Theory of Market Equilibrium under Conditions of Risk', *Journal of Finance*, vol. 19 (September 1964).

2. J. Lintner, 'Security Prices, Risk and Maximal Gains from Diversification', *Journal of Finance*, vol. 20 (December 1965), and 'The Valuation of Risk Assets and the Selection of Risky Investments in Stock Portfolios and Capital Budgets', *Review of Economics and Statistics*, vol. 47 (February 1965).

3. J. Mossin, 'Equilibrium in a Capital Asset Market', *Econometrica* (October 1966).

4. For a discussion of portfolio theory, see W. F. Sharpe, *Portfolio*

Theory and Capital Markets (New York: McGraw-Hill, 1970) or Ryan, *Portfolio Analysis*. Sharpe's book also gives a full description of the C.A.P.M.; only a brief discussion of the theory is given in the current book.

5. An estimating procedure suggested by W. F. Sharpe, 'A Simplified Model for Portfolio Analysis', *Management Science*, vol. IX (January 1963) and subsequently widely adopted.

6. G. Douglas, 'Risk in the Equity Markets: An Empirical Appraisal of Market Efficiency', *Yale Economic Essays* (Spring 1969).

7. Reported in ibid.

8. M. Miller and M. Scholes, 'Rates of Return in Relation to Risk: A Reexamination of Some Recent Findings', in *Studies in the Theory of Capital Markets*, ed. M. Jensen (New York: Praeger, 1972).

9. F. Arditti, 'Another Look at Mutual Fund Performance', *Journal of Financial and Quantitative Analysis* (June 1971).

10. Miller and Scholes, 'Rates of Return in Relation to Risk'.

11. A. Kraus and R. H. Litzenberger, 'Skewness Preference and the Valuation of Risk Assets', *Journal of Finance* (September, 1976).

12. F. Black, M. Jensen and M. Scholes, 'The Capital Asset Pricing Model: Some Empirical Tests', in *Studies in the Theory of Capital Markets*, ed. M. Jensen.

13. This result confirmed earlier findings by M. Jensen, 'Risk, the Pricing of Capital Assets, and the Evaluation of Investment Portfolios', *Journal of Business* (April 1969); M. Blume and I. Friend, 'A New Look at the Capital Asset Pricing Model', *Journal of Finance* (March 1973); and Miller and Scholes, 'Rates of Return in Relation to Risk'.

14. J. G. McDonald, 'Objectives and Performance of Mutual Funds', *Journal of Financial and Quantitative Analysis* (June 1974).

15. This model is similar to that suggested by F. Black, 'Capital Market Equilibrium with Restricted Borrowing', *Journal of Business* (July 1972).

16. E. Fama and J. Macbeth, 'Risk, Return and Equilibrium: Empirical Tests', *Journal of Political Economy* (May–June 1973).

17. W. F. Sharpe, 'Mutual Fund Performance', *Journal of Business*, special supplement, vol. 39 (January 1966).

18. Jensen, 'Risk, the Pricing of Capital Assets'.

19. I. Friend, M. Blume and J. Crockett, *Mutual Funds and other Institutional Investors. A New Perspective*, Twentieth Century Fund Study (New York: McGraw-Hill, 1970).

20. *Institutional Investor Study Report of the Securities and E[xchange] Commission*, 92nd Cong., 1st session (1971).

21. McDonald, 'Objectives and Performance of Mutual Funds'.

22. M. A. Firth, 'The Performance of U.K. Unit Trusts in the period 1965–1975', *Journal of Money, Credit and Banking*, forthcoming.

23. See Jensen, 'Risk, the Pricing of Capital Assets'; H. Levy, 'Portfolio Performance and the Investment Horizon', *Management Science* (August 1972); and P. Cheng and M. Deets, 'Systematic Risk and the Horizon Problem', *Journal of Finance* (March 1971).

24. L. Fisher, 'Good Betas and Bad Betas: How to Tell the Difference', Paper prepared for the Seminar on the Analysis of Security Prices, University of Chicago (November 1971).

25. N. Jacob, 'The Measurement of Systematic Risk for Securities and Portfolios: Some Empirical Results', *Journal of Financial and Quantitative Analysis* (March 1971).

26. M. Blume, 'On the Assessment of Risk', *Journal of Finance* (March 1971).

27. R. Levy, 'On the Short-Term Stationarity of Beta Coefficients', *Financial Analysts Journal* (November–December 1971).

28. W. F. Sharpe and G. Cooper, 'Risk–Return Classes of New York Stock Exchange Common Stocks, 1931–1967', *Financial Analysts Journal* (March–April 1972).

29. J. Aber, 'Multi-Index Linear Assessment Models of Security Return', unpublished D.B.A. dissertation, Harvard Graduate School of Business Administration (1972); and S. Meyers, 'The Stationarity Problem in the Use of the Market Model of Security Price Behaviour', *Accounting Review* (April 1973).

30. See M. Brennan, 'An Approach to the Valuations of Uncertain Income Streams', *Journal of Finance* (June 1973); and S. LeRoy, 'Risk Aversion and the Martingale Property of Stock Prices', *International Economic Review* (June 1973).

31. S. W. Cunningham, 'The Predictability of British Stock Market Prices', *Applied Statistics*, vol. 22, no 3 (1973).

32. See J. Evans and S. Archer, 'Diversification and the Reduction of Dispersion: An Empirical Analysis', *Journal of Finance* (December 1968).

33. Ball and Brown, 'Some Preliminary Findings on the Association between the Earnings of a Firm, Its Industry and the Economy'.

34. W. Beaver, T. P. Kettler and M. Scholes, 'The Association

Between Market Determined and Accounting Determined Risk Measures', *Accounting Review* (October 1970).

35. J. Bildersee, 'The Association Between a Market Determined Measure of Risk and Alternative Measures of Risk', *Accounting Review*, January, 1975.

36. D. Logue and L. Merville, 'Financial Policy and Market Expectations', *Financial Management* (Summer 1972).

37. W. Beaver and J. Manegold, 'The Association Between Market-Determined and Accounting-Determined Measures of Systematic Risk: Some Further Evidence', *Journal of Financial and Quantitative Analysis* (June 1975).

38. W. J. Breen and E. M. Lerner, 'Corporate Financial Strategies and Market Measures of Risk and Return', *Journal of Finance*, vol. 28 (May 1973).

39. N. Gonedes, 'Evidence on the Information Content of Accounting Messages: Accounting Based and Market-Based Estimates of Systematic Risk', *Journal of Financial and Quantitative Analysis* (June 1973), and 'A Note on Accounting-Based and Market-Based Estimates of Systematic Risk', *Journal of Financial and Quantitative Analysis* (June 1975).

40. B. Rosenberg and W. McKibben, 'The Prediction of Systematic and Specific Risk in Common Stocks', *Journal of Financial and Quantitative Analysis* (March 1973).

41. R. Pettit and R. Westerfield, 'A Model of Market Risk', *Journal of Financial and Quantitative Analysis* (March 1972).

42. R. S. Hamada, 'The Effect of the Firm's Capital Structure on the Systematic Risk of Common Stocks', *Journal of Finance*, vol. 27 (May 1972).

43. B. Lev and S. Kunitzky, 'On the Association between Smoothing Measures and the Risk of Common Stocks', *Accounting Review* (April 1974).

44. M. Brenner, 'The Effect of Model Misspecification of Tests of the Efficient Market Hypothesis', *Journal of Finance*, forthcoming.

Chapter 6

1. See E. Fama, 'Efficient Capital Markets. A Review of Theory and Empirical Work', *Journal of Finance* (May 1970).

2. Both P. A. Samuelson, 'Proof That Properly Anticipated

Prices Fluctuate Randomly', *Industrial Management Review*, vol. 6 (Spring 1965), and B. Mandelbrot, 'Forecasts of Future Prices, Unbiased Markets, and Martingale Models', *Journal of Business*, special supplement, vol. 39 (January 1966), have formally proved that independence of successive price changes is consistent with an efficient market.

3. M. Braham, 'The Growing Impact of Stockbrokers' Research', *Money Management and Unitholder* (June 1972).

4. H. C. Wallich, 'What Does the Random Walk Hypothesis Mean to Security Analysts?', *Financial Analysts Journal* (March–April 1968).

5. P. A. Rinfret, 'Investment Managers are Worth Their Keep', *Financial Analysts Journal* (March–April 1968).

6. See Firth, *Investment Analysis*.

7. D. H. Girmes and A. E. Benjamin, 'Random Walk Process for 543 Stocks and Shares Registered on the London Stock Exchange', *Journal of Business Finance and Accounting* (Spring 1975).

Chapter 7

1. C. W. J. Granger, 'Empirical Studies of Capital Markets: A Survey', in *Mathematical Methods in Investments and Finance*, ed. G. P. Szego and K. Shell (Amsterdam: North-Holland, 1972).

2. L. Bachelier, *Théorie de la Spéculation* (Paris: Gauthier-Villars, 1900).

3. H. Working, 'A Random Difference Series for Use in the Analysis of Time Series', *Journal of the American Statistical Association*, vol. 29 (March 1934).

4. A. Cowles and H. Jones, 'Some *A Posteriori* Probabilities in Stock Market Action', *Econometrica*, vol. 5, no. 280 (July 1937).

5. M. G. Kendall, 'The Analysis of Economic Time-Series, Part I: Prices', *Journal of the Royal Statistical Society*, vol. 96, Part I (1953).

6. Working, 'A Random Difference Series'.

7. H. V. Roberts, 'Stock Market "Patterns" and Financial Analysis: Methodological "Suggestions" ', *Journal of Finance*, vol. 14 (March 1959).

8. M. F. M. Osborne, 'Brownian Motion in the Stock Market', *Operations Research*, vol. 7 (March–April 1959).

9. A. B. Moore, 'Some Characteristics of Changes in Common

Stock Prices', in *The Random Character of Stock Market Prices*, ed. P. H. Cootner (M.I.T. Press, 1964).

10. E. F. Fama, 'The Behavior of Stock Market Prices', *Journal of Business* , vol. 38 (January 1965).

11. R. Hagerman and R. Richmond, 'Random Walks, Martingales and the OTC', *Journal of Finance* (September 1973).

12. F. Black and M. Scholes, 'The Valuation of Option Contracts and a Test of Market Efficiency', *Journal of Finance* (May 1972).

13. P. D. Praetz, 'Australian Share Prices and the Random Walk Hypothesis', *Australian Journal of Statistics*, vol. 3 (1969).

14. R. A. Brealey, 'The Distribution and Independence of Successive Rates of Return from the British Equity Market', *Journal of Business Finance* (Summer 1970).

15. Cunningham, 'The Predictability of British Stock Market Prices'.

16. M. M. Dryden, 'A Statistical Study of U.K. Share Prices' *Scottish Journal of Political Economy*, vol. XVII (November 1970).

17. Girmes and Benjamin, 'Random Walk Hypothesis'.

18. C. W. J. Granger and O. Morganstern, *Predictability of Stock Market Prices* (Lexington: Heath, 1970).

19. C. Ying, 'Stock Market Prices and Volume of Sales', *Econometrica* (July 1966).

20. P. Cheng and M. Deets, 'Portfolio Returns and the Random Walk Theory', *Journal of Finance* (March 1971).

21. G. Philippatos and D. Nawrocki, 'The Information Inaccuracy of Stock Market Forecasts: Some New Evidence of Dependence on the New York Stock Exchange', *Journal of Financial and Quantitative Analysis* (June 1973).

22. M. C. Jensen and G. A. Bennington, 'Random Walks and Technical Theories: Some Additional Evidence', *Journal of Finance* vol. 25 (May 1970).

23. S. S. Alexander, 'Price Movements in Speculative Markets: Trends or Random Walks?', *Industrial Management Review*, vol. 2 (May 1961), and 'Price Movements in Speculative Markets: Trends or Random Walks? No. 2', *Industrial Management Review*, vol. 5 (Spring 1964).

24. E. Fama and M. Blume, 'Filter Rules and Stock Market Trading Profits', *Journal of Business*, special supplement, vol. 39 (January 1966).

25. M. M. Dryden, 'Filter Tests of U.K. Share Prices', *Applied Economics*, vol. 1, no. 4 (January 1970).

26. Praetz, 'Australian Share Prices and the Random Walk Hypothesis'.

27. P. Cootner, 'Stock Prices: Random vs. Systematic Changes', *Industrial Management Review*, vol. 3 (Spring 1962).

28. J. C. Van Horne and G. G. C. Parker, 'The Random Walk Theory: An Empirical Test', *Financial Analysts Journal* (November–December 1967).

29. F. E. James, 'Monthly Moving Averages – An Effective Investment Tool?', *Journal of Financial and Quantitative Analysis* (September 1968).

30. J. L. Evans, 'An Analysis of Portfolio Maintenance Strategies', *Journal of Finance* (June 1970).

31. H. A. Latané and W. E. Young, 'Tests of Portfolio Building Rules', *Journal of Finance*, vol. xxiv, no. 4 (September 1969).

32. See, for example, R. Levy, 'Relative Strength as a Criterion for Investment Selection', *Journal of Finance*, vol. 22 (Dec. 1967).

33. Jensen and Bennington, 'Random Walks and Technical Theories'.

34. See, for example, J. McWilliams, 'Prices, Earnings and P. E. Ratios', *Financial Analysts Journal* (May–June 1966); P. Miller and E. Widman, 'Price Performance Outlook for High and Low P. E. Stocks', 1966 Stock and Bond Issue, *Commercial and Financial Chronicle*, vol. 29 (September 1966); K. Homa and D. Jaffee, 'The Supply of Money and Common Stock Prices', *Journal of Finance* (December 1971); M. Zweig, 'An Investor Expectations Stock Price Predictive Model Using Closed-End Fund Premiums', *Journal of Finance* (March 1973); and S. Basu, 'Investment Performance of Common Stocks in Relation to Their Price–Earnings Ratios: A Test of the Efficient Market Hypothesis', *Journal of Finance*, forthcoming.

35. Sharpe, 'A Simplified Model for Portfolio Analysis'. Recent work by Black, Jensen and Scholes, 'The Capital Asset Pricing Model', and Fama and Macbeth, 'Risk, Return and Equilibrium', have derived better explanatory models of share price behaviour although these have, as yet, not been heavily utilised in research studies (see pp. 97–98).

36. B. F. King, 'Market and Industry Factors in Stock Price Behavior', *Journal of Business*, special supplement, vol. 39 (January 1966).

37. P. R. Draper, 'Industry Influence on Share Price Variability', *Journal of Business Finance and Accounting*, (Summer 1975).

38. E. Fama, L. Fisher, M. Jensen and R. Roll, 'The Adjustment of Stock Prices to New Information', *International Economic Review*, vol. 10 (February 1969).

39. See Ball, 'Changes in Accounting Techniques and Stock Prices', for a discussion.

40. Fama, Fisher, Jensen and Roll, 'The Adjustment of Stock Prices to New Information'.

41. K. B. Johnson, 'Stock Splits and Price Change', *Journal of Finance*, vol. xxi (December 1966).

42. F. J. Finn, 'Stock Splits: Prior and Subsequent Price Relationships', *Journal of Business Finance and Accounting* (Spring 1974).

43. M. A. Firth, 'An Empirical Examination of the Applicability of Adopting the AICPA and NYSE Regulations on Free Share Distributions in the U.K.', *Journal of Accounting Research* (Spring 1973), *The Incidence and Impact of Capitalisation Issues*, Occasional Paper No. 3, (Institute of Chartered Accountants in England and Wales, 1974), and 'An Empirical Investigation of the Impact of the Announcement of Capitalisation Issues on Share Prices', *Journal of Business Finance and Accounting* (Spring 1977).

44. R. Pettit, 'Dividend Announcements, Security Performance and Capital Market Efficiency', *Journal of Finance* (December 1972).

45. R. Watts, 'The Information Content of Dividends', *Journal of Business* (April 1973).

46. A. Kraus and H. Stoll, 'Price Impacts of Block Trading in the New York Stock Exchange', *Journal of Finance*, vol. xxvii (June 1972).

47. M. S. Scholes, 'The Market for Securities: Substitution versus Price Pressure and the Effects of Information on Share Prices', *Journal of Business*, vol. 45 (April 1972).

48. R. Waud, 'Public Interpretation of Federal Reserve Discount Rate Changes: Evidence on the Announcement Effect', *Econometrica* (March 1970).

49. R. Ball and P. Brown, 'An Empirical Evaluation of Accounting Income Numbers', *Journal of Accounting Research* (Autumn 1968); and Beaver, 'Market Prices, Financial Ratios, and the Prediction of Failure'.

50. Brown and Kennelly, 'The Informational Content of Quarterly Earnings'; R. May, 'The Influence of Quarterly Earnings Announcements on Investor Decisions as Reflected in Common

Stock Price Changes', Empirical Research in Accounting: Selected Studies, 1971, *Journal of Accounting Research*, supplement (1971); and R. Jordan, 'An Empirical Investigation of the Adjustment of Stock Prices to New Quarterly Earnings Information', *Journal of Financial and Quantitative Analysis* (September 1973).

51. See, for example, D. Patz and J. Boatsman, 'Accounting Principle Formulation in an Efficient Markets Environment', *Journal of Accounting Research* (Autumn 1972); E. E. Comiskey, 'Market Response to Changes in Depreciation Accounting', *Accounting Review* (April 1971); T. Archibald, 'Stock Market Reaction to the Depreciation Switch-Back', *Accounting Review* (January 1972); R. Kaplan and R. Roll, 'Investor Evaluation of Accounting Information: Some Empirical Evidence', *Journal of Business* (April 1972); Ball, 'Changes in Accounting Techniques and Stock Prices', and S. Sunder, 'Relationships Between Accounting Changes and Stock Prices: Problems of Measurement and Some Empirical Evidence', Empirical Research in Accounting: Selected Studies, 1973, *Journal of Accounting Research*, supplement (1973).

52. G. Foster, 'Stock Market Reaction to Estimates of Earnings per Share by Company Officials', *Journal of Accounting Research* (Spring 1973).

53. Jones and Litzenberger, 'Quarterly Earnings Reports and Intermediate Stock Price Trends'.

54. C. Jones, 'Earnings Trends and Investment Selection', *Financial Analysts Journal*, vol. 25 (March 1970).

55. M. A. Firth, 'The Information Content of Large Investment Holdings', *Journal of Finance* (December 1975).

56. Firth, *Share Prices and Mergers*.

57. Firth, 'The Impact of Earnings Announcements on the Share Price Behaviour of Similar Type Firms'.

58. Firth, 'An Empirical Investigation of the Impact of the Announcement of Capitalisation Issues on Share Prices.

59. M. D. Fitzgerald, 'An Investigation into the Relationship Between Information Flows and Stock Market Prices', Ph.D. thesis, Manchester Business School (1974).

60. V. Niederhoffer and M. F. M. Osborne, 'Market Making and Reversal on the Stock Exchange', *Journal of the American Statistical Association*, vol. 61 (December 1966).

61. J. H. Lorie and V. Niederhoffer, 'Predictive and Statistical

Properties of Insider Trading', *Journal of Law and Economics*, vol. 11 (April 1968).

62. S. P. Pratt and C. W. De Vere, 'Relationship between Insider Trading and Rates of Return for N.Y.S.E. Common Stocks, 1960–1966', Paper presented for the Seminar on the Analysis of Security Prices, University of Chicago (May 1968), reprinted in *Modern Developments in Investment Management*, ed. J. Lorie and R. A. Brealey (New York: Praeger, 1972).

63. J. Jaffe, 'Special Information and Insider Trading', *Journal of Business* (July 1974).

64. D. Collins, 'SEC Product-Line Reporting and Market Efficiency', *Journal of Financial Economics* (June, 1975).

65. See, for example, I. Friend, F. Brown, E. Herman and D. Vickers, *A Study of Mutual Funds*, prepared for the Securities and Exchange Commission by the Securities Research Unit, Wharton School of Finance and Commerce, University of Pennsylvania (Washington D.C.: U.S. Government Printing Office, 1962); Sharpe 'Mutual Fund Performance'; M. Jensen, 'The Performance of Mutual Funds in the Period 1945–64', *Journal of Finance* (May 1968); Friend, Blume and Crockett, *Mutual Funds and Other Institutional Investors*; J. Williamson, 'Measuring Mutual Fund Performance', *Financial Analysts Journal'* (November–December 1972); and McDonald, 'Objectives and Performance of Mutual Funds'.

66. Firth, 'The Performance of U.K. Unit Trusts'.

67. See, for example, M. A. Firth, 'The Performance of Share Recommendations Made By Investment Analysts and the Effects on Market Efficiency', *Journal of Business Finance*, vol. 4 (Summer 1972); J. G. Cragg and B. G. Malkiel, 'The Consensus and Accuracy of Some Predictions of the Growth of Corporate Earnings', *Journal of Finance*, vol. 23, no. 1 (1968); and E. J. Elton and M. J. Gruber, 'Earnings Estimates and the Accuracy of Expectations Data', *Management Science*, vol. 18 (April 1972).

68. See, for example, Kendall, 'The Analysis of Economic Time-Series'.

69. Mandelbrot, 'Forecasts of Future Prices, Unbiased Markets, and Martingale Models'.

70. Fama, 'The Behavior of Stock Market Prices'.

71. Later studies by various researchers confirmed these findings. This also applies to U.K. and Australian data; see, respectively, Brealey, 'The Distribution and Independence of Successive Rates

of Return from the British Equity Market', and P. D. Praetz, 'The Distribution of Share Price Changes', *Journal of Business* (January 1972).

72. J. Fried, 'Forecasting and Probability Distributions for Models of Portfolio Selection', *Journal of Finance*, vol. xxv (June 1970).

73. See, for example, Fama, 'Efficient Capital Markets'.

Chapter 8

1. Ball and Brown, 'An Empirical Evaluation of Accounting Income Numbers'.

2. P. Brown, 'The Impact of the Annual Net Profit Report on the Stock Market', *Australian Accountant*, vol. 40 (1970).

3. Beaver, 'Market Prices, Financial Ratios, and the Prediction of Failure'.

4. B. Lev and B. Yahalomi, 'The Effects of Corporate Financial Statements on the Israeli Stock Exchange', *Management International Review*, vol. 12, nos. 2–3 (1972).

5. Brown and Kennelly, 'The Informational Content of Quarterly Earnings'.

6. May, 'The Influence of Quarterly Earnings Announcements on Investor Decisions as Reflected in Common Stock Price Changes'

7. J. Kiger, 'An Empirical Investigation of NYSE Volume and Price Reactions to the Announcement of Quarterly Earnings', *Journal of Accounting Research* (Spring 1972).

8. A Martin, 'An Empirical Test of the Relevance of Accounting Information for Investment Decisions', Empirical Research in Accounting: Selected Studies, 1971, *Journal of Accounting Research*, supplement, vol. 9 (1971).

9. Firth, 'The Impact of Earnings Announcements on the Share Price Behaviour of Similar Type Firms'.

10. T. R. Dyckman, 'On the Investment Decision', *Accounting Review*, vol. 39 (April 1964).

11. R. E. Jensen, 'An Experimental Design for Study of Effects of Accounting Variations in Decision Making', *Journal of Accounting Research*, vol. 4 (Autumn 1966).

12. W. J. Bruns, Jr, 'Inventory Valuation and Management Decisions', *Accounting Review*, vol. 40 (April 1965).

13. M. E. Barrett, 'Accounting for Intercorporate Investments:

A Behavioral Field Experiment', Empirical Research in Accounting: Selected Studies, 1971, *Journal of Accounting Research*, supplement, vol. 9 (1971).

14. C. P. Bonini, *Simulation of Information and Decision Systems in the Firm* (Englewood Cliffs, N.J.: Prentice-Hall, 1969); E. F. Brigham, 'The Effects of Alternative Depreciation Policies on Reported Profits', *Accounting Review*, vol. 43 (January 1968); E. E. Comiskey and F. A. Mlynarczyk, 'Recognition of Income by Finance Companies', *Accounting Review*, vol. 43 (1968); and M. N. Greenball, 'Evaluation of the Usefulness to Investors of Different Accounting Estimators of Earnings', Empirical Research in Accounting: Selected Studies, 1968, *Journal of Accounting Research*, supplement, vol. 6 (1968).

15. John L. O'Donnell, 'Relationships Between Reported Earnings and Stock Prices in the Electric Utility Industry', *Accounting Review* (January 1965).

16. John L. O'Donnell, 'Further Observations on Reported Earnings and Stock Prices', *Accounting Review* (July 1968).

17. E. L. Summers, 'Observation of Effects of Using Alternative Reporting Practices', *Accounting Review*, vol. 43 (April 1968).

18. F. A. Mlynarczyk, 'An Empirical Study of Accounting Methods and Stock Prices', Empirical Research in Accounting: Selected Studies, 1969, *Journal of Accounting Research*, supplement, vol. 7 (1969).

19. Comiskey, 'Market Response to Changes in Depreciation Accounting'.

20. N. Gonedes, 'The Significance of Selected Accounting Procedures: A Statistical Test', Empirical Research in Accounting', Selected Studies, 1969, *Journal of Accounting Research*, supplement (1969).

21. Archibald, 'Stock Market Reaction to the Depreciation Switch-Back'.

22. Kaplan and Roll, 'Investor Evaluation of Accounting Information'.

23. See Ball, 'Changes in Accounting Techniques and Stock Prices'.

24. Ibid.

25. Sunder, 'Relationships Between Accounting Changes and Stock Prices'.

26. R. C. Morris, 'Evidence of the Impact of Inflation Accounting on Share Prices', *Accounting and Business Research* (Spring 1975).

27. See W. Frank, 'A Study of the Predictive Significance of Two Income Measures', *Journal of Accounting Research* (1969); R. A. Samuelson, 'Prediction and Price-Level Adjustment', *Journal of Accounting Research* (1972); Greenball, 'Evaluation of the Usefulness to Investors of Different Accounting Estimators of Earnings'; J. K. Simmons and J. Gray, 'An Investigation of the Effect of Differing Accounting Frameworks on the Prediction of Net Income', *Accounting Review*, vol. 44 (October 1969); and E. V. McIntyre, 'Current Cost Financial Statements and Common Stock Investment Decisions', *Accounting Review* (1973).

28. For a discussion of the predictive ability criterion, see for example N. Gonedes, 'Efficient Capital Markets and External Accounting', *Accounting Review* (January 1972); R. May and G. Sundem, 'Cost of Information and Security Prices: Market Association Tests for Accounting Policy Decisions', *Accounting Review* (January 1973); H. Bierman, 'The Implications of Efficient Markets and the Capital Asset Pricing Model to Accounting', *Accounting Review* (July 1974); M. N. Greenball, 'The Predictive-Ability Criterion: Its Relevance in Evaluating Accounting Data', *Abacus*, vol. 7 (June 1971); W. Beaver, 'The Behavior of Security Prices and Its Implication for Accounting Research (Methods)', *Accounting Review*, supplement (1972); and 'Implications of Security Price Research for Accounting: A Reply to Bierman', *Accounting Review* (July 1974); B. Carsberg, A. Hope and R. W. Scapens, 'The Objectives of Published Accounting Reports', *Accounting and Business Research* (Summer 1974), and 'The Objectives of Published Accounting Reports: Reply to a Comment', *Accounting and Business Research* (Spring 1975); K. V. Peasnell, *The Usefulness of Accounting Information to Investors*, Occasional Paper No. 1 (I.C.R.A., 1973), and 'Objectives of Published Accounting Reports: A Comment', *Accounting and Business Research* (Winter 1974); and W. J. Kenley and G. T. Staubus, *Objectives and Concepts of Financial Statements* (Accounting Research Foundation, 1972).

29. *Trueblood Report, Objectives of Financial Statements* (A.I.C.P.A., 1973).

30. *Corporate Report* (Institute of Chartered Accountants in England and Wales, 1975).

Index